Woven Prayers
A Prayer Shawl Ministry Handbook

EVELYN RAINEY

ISBN-13: 978-1-946469-41-0

Sheltering Tree . Earth, LLC Publishing
PO Box 973, Eagle Lake, FL 33839

ShelteringTree.Earth

DEDICATION

For all those who look at a skein of yarn and a crochet hook and believe they can make the world a better place; and then do.

CONTENTS

ACKNOWLEDGMENTS

I would like to thank all the women who taught me to crochet and to master the art – those who taught me face-to-face when I was a child, and all the authors who wrote books and magazines and produced videos about crochet.

I would especially like to thank all the members of the McLeod Presbyterian Prayer Shawl Ministry who helped me write this book by working through all these issues and victories every other Tuesday night for five years from 2008 to 2013.

INTRODUCTION

Exodus 35:35

He has filled them with skill to do all kinds of work
as craftsmen, designers, embroiderers in blue,
purple and scarlet yarn and fine linen, and weavers
– all of them master craftsmen and designers.

I love blue, purple and scarlet yarn! I have crocheted most of my life, and when I found out that there were women across the nation who were forming Prayer Shawl Ministries I became so excited; I started one at my church. We meet every two weeks and each week, I send an email to the members with suggestions for uplifting hymns, instructional scripture and encouraging words.

There are forty-one lessons in this book divided into three areas: personal relationship with God, interpersonal relationships with others, and a ministerial relationship with the world. Each one weaves together the art of crocheting and the love of God. There are eight crochet patterns, this introduction, and a resource guide including steps on how to form your own Prayer Shawl Ministry. The scriptures in this devotional are from the *English Standard Version* of the **Bible** published by Crossway and from the New International Version as listed on Biblegateway.com unless otherwise stated.

In the center of this book is a devotional on the most important aspect of prayer shawl ministries: Prayer.

So, if God has filled you with a love for crocheting and knitting, pull out those blue, purple and scarlet yarns and those crochet hooks and knitting needles and join me. This handbook for Prayer Shawl Ministries is for you.

PERSONAL RELATIONSHIP WITH GOD

STITCH BY STITCH

Luke 8:14-15

The seed that fell among thorns stands for those who hear, but as they go on their way they are choked by life's worries, riches and pleasures, and they do not mature. But the seed on good soil stands for those with a noble and good heart, who hear the word, retain it, and by persevering produce a crop.

I get so excited when I find a new pattern. The picture is breathtaking, and the completed work conveys an essence of warmth, beauty, and homemade bliss.

"I can make that," I assure myself.

I buy new yarn especially for this project (because none of the hundreds of skeins in my spare bedroom would be "just right").

I fix a pot of tea and settle in my armchair -- with my dog at my feet and my cats on the chair's threadbare arms. And I begin.

The first step for any crochet project is universal: chain X number of stitches. Got it.

Then come the secret codes: *DC, HDC, decrease next 3 CH, * SC in next 5, chain 7 * Repeat for 6 rows, Turn.*

I crochet diligently for an hour. My tea grows cold. My dog snores; my cats purr. However, what I hold between my hands looks nothing like the pattern's picture.

I want it finished now. I want my crochet hook to turn into a magic wand and whisk the yarn into immediate completion. I want to wrap this glorious piece of handiwork in rustling tissue paper and send it to a friend. Now.

But I have eleven skeins and three pages of instructions left...

Life is like a crochet pattern. The Master knows what my life will be in completion and shows me the beauty it can become. But I have to live stitch by stitch, skein by skein, and meticulously follow the directions given. I have to trust that the directions are true and accurate. I have to have faith that what I am working toward will be useful and beautiful -- if not now, then definitely when I am finished with it.

I have to live stitch by stitch.

Dear Master,
Help us to see beyond the everyday steps to the glory
you have provided for us. And for those times when
we are blinded by impatience, help us to just trust
You to place our feet where You want them to go.
Help us to live day by day, step by step, and stitch by
stitch. Amen.

Your personal notes:

THE COLORS YOU GIVE AWAY

Psalm 19:14
*May the words of my mouth and the meditation of
my heart be pleasing in your sight, O Lord, my Rock
and my Redeemer.*

One of the first prayer shawls I made came from a collection of leftover balls of yarn in army camouflage colors. I ran out of this yarn before the shawl was big enough, so I finished the last three rows in black. It matched. My mother told me it was hideous, and she was right. I cannibalized the shawl. The black yarn became fringe on a serape. The camouflage yarn became baby booties for the Teen Parent Centers.

We have Yarn Angels at my church who religiously scour every garage sale and bring my Prayer Shawl Ministry boxes of yarn. I love these Angels dearly and am so grateful for their generosity. Sometimes however, inside the boxes are yarns of colors that will never be put to good use -- for good reason: they are dreadful.

Each color has its own spiritual meaning. On a color wheel, each color has its own partners and adversaries. Advertisers, clothes designers, and psychologists know this. Primary colors (pure red, yellow, and blue) recall childhood innocence. Gray, blue, and black blend well and give the viewer a sense of security. Neon colors are meant to be glaring. White represents purity just as black alludes to death. When I'm excited, I wear reds, oranges, and yellows. When I feel depressed, I tend to be attracted to dark colors. When I feel healthy, I choose earthy colors. When I feel calm, I surround myself in peaceful blues.

The recipients of my shawls will wear the colors I choose for them. I think about what I want to wrap them in: death or serenity, security or despair, jazziness or innocence.

The recipients of my words and actions should be treated the same way. I try to choose my words and actions as carefully as I choose my yarn. They are what my listeners and observers will take away with them.

Dear Father, let the words that I say, the actions I take, and the works I do leave the people around me surrounded by Your grace and Your joy and Your hope. Amen.

Your personal notes:

CHOOSING THE RIGHT YARN

Psalm 139: 13-14
*For you created my inmost being; you knit me
together in my mother's womb.
I praise you because I am fearfully and wonderfully
made; your words are wonderful, I know that full
well.*

I get all glazy-eyed at a craft store. I stand amazed and awed by the vast array of colors, weights, materials, and plies of all the yarns before me. I probably drool, too.

I am an adventurous crotcheter. I see a fluffy chenille and think, what if I used it for a basket weave pattern? I admire the all organic 100% cotton yarn and wonder how it would work for a summer skirt. Sometimes it works. Sometimes it doesn't.

Lessons I have learned from these experiments:

- chunky yarn should not be used for large projects requiring small hooks
- fuzzy yarn works better as a knitted project because crochet hooks get caught in the knaps
- wool tugs at my heritage and makes me yearn imaginatively for fishing villages and peat fires. However, wool really does not work well in the tropics
- when the contents state "4% other", it will shrink, stretch, fade, and/or itch
- baby yarn is fabulous – soft, gentle colors, washable -- but cannot replace chunky yarn nor vice versa in order to yield an article in the correct and expected proportions

People are like yarn. Each has its own weight, ply, and content. Each should be used in patterns which fit them. The differences between yarn -- and people -- depend on their content and how they were twisted and twined. I think I'm solid, all natural, tan cotton four ply yarn. Probably the best pattern for my life may be to become a potholder. People need potholders. Potholders protect and preserve. They are washable and always smell of sugar cookies. If I spend my whole life trying to become a baby blanket or a chemotherapy cap, I will be useless. Four-ply is too big for a baby blanket and cotton is not warm enough for a chemotherapy cap.

I trust God to weave me into a suitable pattern for my life. God knows my fabric content. He knows the appropriate use for me. After all, He made me.

Dear Lord,
Let me not just be content with the pattern you have
chosen for my life. Let me be ecstatic about it. Amen.

Your personal notes:

A GOOD PAIR OF SCISSORS

Philippians 1: 9-11
*And this is my prayer: that your love may abound
more and more in knowledge and depth of insight, so
that you may be able to discern what is best and may
be pure and blameless until the day of Christ, filled
with the fruit of righteousness that comes through
Jesus Christ – to the glory and praise of God.*

There was nothing else I could do. I had jiggled and pushed and used a needle and my fingernails and spent too much time gently tweezing it this way and that -- to no avail. I was going to have to cut the yarn.

A good pair of scissors slices through the yarn as opposed to chewing it. The ends can be tied together without fear of fraying and the project can continue.

I once tried to make a multicolored granny square without cutting any yarn. The colors would be used repeatedly throughout the afghan, so why mar it with tiny clusters of knots and flailing cut ends? I eventually realized I was spending more time untangling the skeins than crocheting the afghan.

Some patterns cannot be successfully completed without cutting the yarn and tying it off. My baby booties are a good example. The foot part ends at the center of the sole. The anklet has to be started at the top side of the ruffle. There is no way to complete the bootie without ending one phase and beginning another.

Don't be afraid of using scissors. They are necessary. Learn to let go, tie off, and begin again. Some patterns call for it. Some situations in life do, too.

My Jesus,
Help me to let go when it is time to let go. Help me
to turn my back and walk away when it is time for me
to leave. Don't let me cling to things that are not
good for me. Help me to let go, help me to let go, help
me to let go. Amen.

Your personal notes:

FOLLOWING DIRECTIONS

John 21: 15-17
... Jesus said, "Feed my lambs." ... Jesus said,
"Take care of my sheep." ... Jesus said, "Feed my
sheep."

As an elementary teacher, I learned that directions should be stated in positive terms. "Don't run!" should be said, "Walk." "Stop talking!" should be, "Listen and follow directions so that you can do your work." As a teacher of crochet, I try to give positive directions, too. "You're going to jab your eye out!" becomes, "Loosen the tension on the yarn so your hook will slide easily."

Another trick I learned as a teacher is that if I gently repeat the exact phrase and ignore the excuses, the student will eventually comply with the directions. "Do a double crochet in that chain space."

To which the student bleats, "But there's not enough room in that loop."

I repeat, "Do a double crochet in the **chain space**." And I show her where the chain space is.

In the chain space, the student does a single crochet and an extra three chains at the top.

"Do a **double crochet** in the chain space," I again direct. And I show her how to do a double crochet.

Following directions can be just as difficult as giving them. I have to trust and respect the person telling me to follow directions. I also have to see a purpose for the directions. In crochet or knitting, the final purpose is clear – there is a picture of the finished product on the front page. But the clusters of directions can seem overwhelming. (Loop your hook under the yarn, swirl it around once, push the hook through the anchor loop. Swirl the hook under the yarn at your left pointer finger and grab it, pull it through the anchor loop. Swirl the hook around the yarn again and pull it through the two loops on your hook. Swirl the hook again and pull it through the remaining two loops on your hook. That's a double crochet stitch. Now do 159 more on this one row of 80 rows.)

I have seen grown women throw tantrums when being given directions. It's not pretty. Shouts of, "I can't!" "It's not going that way!" "This is stupid!" and other less nice declinations of ability lead to only one end result: the shawl will never be completed.

Take a deep breath. It always helps to take a deep breath. I am not sure why, but it does. So take a deep breath and gently repeat your directions.

Even Jesus had to tell Peter three times.

Making a shawl is a way of feeding Jesus's sheep and taking care of His lambs. The directions are simple, "Make a shawl." Follow the directions . . . If you love Him, then you will do it.

Well God, you know how stubborn I am and that I'm not very good at all of this. But please Lord, be patient with me. Go ahead and repeat your directions. Keep telling me what to do, because I do love you, God. I want to follow your directions. Help me feed your sheep. Amen.

Your personal notes:

LOAVES AND FISHES PRAYER SHAWL

John 14:6
Jesus answered, "I am the way and the truth and the life. No one comes to the Father except through me.

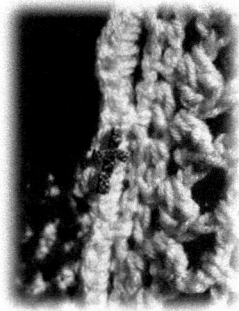

A prayer shawl is woven, knitted, or crocheted specifically as a gift for someone else. It can be triangular, rectangular, or crescent. It should be made of hypo-allergenic yarn, but can be made from wool, silk, cotton, bamboo or acrylic threads. It is just a shawl - with one exceptional difference: it is prayed over and offered as a woven prayer.

No one is a stranger to grief. No one is a stranger to sorrow or despair; to mourning, disaster or stressful changes of life. When someone who is going through any one of life's multitudinous tragedies receives a prayer shawl, they receive something comforting with which to wrap themselves. They also wrap themselves in the prayers, scriptures. and kindness that has imbued the yarn during the shawl's creation.

Yes, I did say the yarn is imbued with prayers. In Mark 5:25-34, the woman was healed just by touching the hem of Jesus's Prayer Shawl. It was imbued with healing powers. The same miraculous power can flow from God, through your heart and fingers, and into the yarn of the shawl (or anything else you pray over). From there, it can bless and comfort the shawl's recipient.

No one is a stranger to grief. But no one is a stranger to joy, either. Don't forget to imbue the prayer shawl with joy, too.

I designed this Loaves and Fishes Prayer Shawl based on the miracle of the loaves and fishes. It is triangular in shape, and soft and comforting in style. Worn with jeans and a T or an evening gown, or anything in between, this shawl is warm without being hot, and goes anywhere.

The pattern uses DC sets to represent loaves of bread and chains to represent fish nets. The Miracle of the Loaves and Fishes (Mark 6:35-44, Matthew 14:16-21 and Luke 12-17) reminds us that there is abundance in all things. Yes, at certain times in our lives, we seem to have an abundance of sorrow, grief, and illness. But we also have an abundance of joy.

Basic Pattern

Loaves

2DC in each chain space.

Chain one between the 2DC sets.

Fish

First row: chain 5, sc in chain space

Second and following rows: chain 5, sc in middle of chain

5 space below.

Center:

Use for both loaves and fishes patterns

2DC, chain 2, 2DC in the center 2chain space.

First of each row:

DC in base of the turning chain, chain 1, 2DC

Loaves: continue pattern chain 1, 2DC in chain space,

chain 1

Fish: chain 3, sc in chain space below, 5 chain – continue

the patterns of chain 5, sc into chain below.

End of each row

Loaves: 2DC into last chain space, DC into top of last

stitch, then DC between the columns of the last 2 DC, chain 2, turn

Fishes: When you are two sets from the edge, chain 3

instead of 5, 2DC into last chain space, DC into top of last stitch,

then DC between the columns of the last 2 DC, chain 2, turn

For Mercerized cotton thread or 3-weight, do 10 rows of loaves, the 10 rows of fishes, and repeat until it is the length required. For anything heavier, do 5 rows of each.

Borders:

Along the flat top side – use 2 or 3 hdc in each column (last stitch along the tops)

Along the 2 sides connected by the center set, try various ones:

For a frilly edge (as used in the yellow mercerized cotton thread): 5 DC in one stitch, skip 2 stitches, sc in third stitch skip 2 stitches. Repeat until the center, where you will put 7 DC in the center chain space. Repeat the first part until the end.

For a pointed effect (as used in the earth-tones acrylic): Down the sides: (sc, hdc, dc, tc, picot, tc, dc, hdc, sc) as a repeat – one in each stitch – through both loops. In the center, adjust the stitches so that the tc are in the center chain space. Do 2tc, picot, 2tc in the chain space. The reflect your adjustments until you can return to the (sc, hdc, dc, tc, picot, tc, dc, hdc, sc) pattern.

Slip stitch to close. Weave in.

Note: picot is chain 3, sc stitch in third from hook. Advanced crocheters may use Clones Knot instead of a picot.

For a solid effect (as used in the brown linen thread): continue the Hdc in each stitch.

Holy Spirit,
There are so many threes in our lives: birth, life,
death; father, son, holy spirit; maiden, mother,
wisdom; yes, no, maybe. As the recipient wears this
shawl, please help her understand that there are at
least two solutions to every problem. Let her rely
on you to help solve them.
Amen

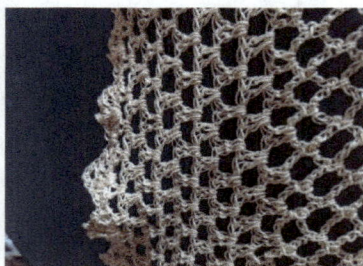

ENVIRONMENTAL FACTORS

John 13:34

"A new commandment I give you: Love one another. As I have loved you, so you must love one another. By this all men will know that you are my disciples, if you love one another."

Moonbeam is utterly fascinated by my shawls. She supervises the path of the yarn, kneads the skeins, and snuggles into the folds of the material. She means no harm. But she leaves behind tiny strands of fur which become incorporated into the shawls. Moonbeam - my mostly Siamese cat - is part of my household, as is my Labrador Daisy and their orange tabby Gilbert. They are all part of my life and also add pieces of themselves to the shawls.

I store my shawls during the weeks between the meetings in a huge plastic bag into which I drop scented soap. The stored shawls emerge smelling of floral bouquets, and sometimes still bear traces of Moonbeam, Daisy and Gilbert.

People who smoke exude a scent through their pores, so I am glad -- not only for the shawls' recipients' sake -- that I no longer smoke. People who wear strong perfumes also add their own essence to the shawls and yarns donated to the ministry. Yarn often comes to us smelling of wherever it was stored: moldy closets, dusty attics, mouse-infested garages. Sometimes they are infused with cedar, mothballs, or lavender.

Fur and odors can be washed away, but the awareness that the things in your life cling to everything you do should not be forgotten.

Heavenly Father, forgive those who gossip about me. I know I did some really wicked things in my life, and I'll never be able to walk down the street without someone whispering behind my back. I did those things. You and I have discussed those things and You have forgiven me. Between us, those things do not exist anymore. But the world doesn't look at me the same way You do. Help me to be the kind of person that from here on out, only bits and pieces of Your kingdom will cling to my works. Thank you. Amen.

Your personal notes:

MISTAKES

Romans 8:18 - 21

*I consider that our present sufferings are not worth
comparing with the glory that will be revealed in us.
The creation waits in eager expectation for the sons
of God to be revealed. For the creation was
subjected to frustration, not by its own choice, but
by the will of the one who subjected it, in hope, that
the creation itself will be liberated from its bondage
to decay and brought into the glorious freedom of
the children of God.*

It is three o'clock in the morning and my phone rings. On
the other end comes an anguished cry, "It's ruined! It won't work!
I don't know what to do!"

The answer flows easily from my lips, "Go back to the last
correct stitch."

The listener however is usually reluctant to unravel her yarn.
She wants to redesign the pattern to incorporate the mistake.
"Maybe no one will notice."

Mistakes left to their own devices eventually ruin the entire
piece. No matter how many rows you have stitched since the
mistake, it will not heal and it will not disappear. You must go back
and fix it. Unravel beyond the mistake. Re-read the directions. Call
a friend and ask for advice. Sometimes you may have to cut a chunk
of yarn away and reconnect the ends.

The important thing is not to give up. Learn from your
mistakes, improve your skills, adjust your actions, re-read your

directions, and go back to the point where you were on the right path.

Do the same with mistakes in your life; and allow others to do the same in their lives.

Dear Jesus,
I'm sorry. I don't know how it happened, but it did.
Help me find my way back to You. Keep my feet on
your path. Amen.

Your personal notes:

RHYTHM

Ecclesiastes 3:1-8
There is a time for everything,
And a season for every activity under heaven:
A time to be born and a time to die,
A time to plant and a time to uproot,
A time to kill and a time to heal,
A time to tear down and a time to build,
A time to weep and a time to laugh,
A time to mourn and a time to dance,
A time to scatter stones and a time to gather them,
A time to embrace and a time to refrain,
A time to search and a time to give up,
A time to keep and a time to throw away
A time to tear and a time to mend,
A time to be silent and a time to speak,
A time to love and a time to hate,
A time for war and a time for peace.

Abide with me, fast falls the eventide, I hum softly and double crochet my way along the side of my triangular shawl. The rhythm of the song matches the motions of my hands. The song soothes me; the shawl grows.

Some stitches call for faster songs. *I Must Tell Jesus* works well for chains and single crochets. *Deep River* and *Amazing Grace* accompanies more intricate or elaborate stitches.

Different stitches call for different rhythms.

I crochet much faster than most people, so my rhythm is swifter than theirs. I don't match my rhythm to anyone around me.

I have my own patterns to follow and my own ability to guide me. Luckily I have memorized enough hymns, scriptures, and creeds to keep me going as I work through easy, difficult, and challenging stitches. Before I know it, the project is complete.

There is a rhythm to life as well. The rhythm flies swiftly through easy situations, steadily through harder patches, and solidly through times of turmoil and despair. I don't expect anyone to match my rhythm for more than a short time; they have a different pattern to follow. When one song ends, I begin another. I sing, pray, and recite my way through life.

God, it's really hard right now. I don't know that I can do this. Please, sweet Jesus, give me the strength I need to face what lies ahead. Everything was so easy just yesterday! I trust that things will be easier in a little while. Just don't let me stop loving You. Don't let me stop serving You. It is so tough right now. But You are my strength. I know You will see me through. Thank you. Amen.

Your personal notes:

WASHING INSTRUCTIONS

1 John 1:9

*If we confess our sins, He is faithful and just and
will forgive us our sins and purify us from all
unrighteousness.*

It's going to happen. It's going to get dirty. Whether it is the fluffy white baby blanket or the bright yellow chemo cap or the lavender and azure prayer shawl; it is going to get dirty.

So, wash it.

Put it in the sink filled with cold water and gentle soap or dump it in a washing machine with harsh detergent. The solution to a dirty article is to wash it.

Most articles will come out clean and whole. Sometimes, the washing process changes the shape or size of the article, but the dirt is gone.

Make sure the recipients of your gifts understand that getting dirty is a normal part of use. Make sure the recipients also understand that dirty things can be washed clean.

I live in the world and often get dirty. The Bible calls this dirt *sin*. I smirk. I complain. I criticize. I forget to pray. I judge. I covet. I get angry. I doubt. I worry. The list goes on and on. I get spiritually dirty.

Luckily, I can be washed clean by Jesus. It's very simple. I confess my sins, I apologize for doing them, I ask for guidance in avoiding them the next time, and Jesus forgives me. Sometimes, the process changes me. But always, I come clean.

I really goofed today, Lord! I am so sorry! Help me to find a better way to deal with that situation. I know there may be repercussions for what I did; let me face those without whining. Forgive me. Amen.

Your personal notes:

WHY DO YOU NEVER RUN OUT OF YARN?

2 Corinthians 9:8

And God is able to bless you abundantly, so that in
all things at all times, having all that you need, you
will abound in every good work.

You've noticed it, haven't you? The bags and totes with donated yarn never seem to diminish. Why do you suppose that is?

Donating yarn to this ministry is such a generous thing. I appreciate every skein and ball that comes our way.

My ladies take enough yarn to make a shawl or a dozen caps or a baby blanket at least once every meeting.

And yet the yarn totes are never emptied.

Like God's love – there will never be an end to it.

King of Heaven,
How often have you opened your storehouses to me
when I needed just a little of something to give to
someone in need. Like the fish and the loaves of
bread, there is abundance of things shared. Your
love will never run dry. Your grace is sufficient for
all things. You amaze me, God. Thank you!
Amen

Your personal notes:

INTERPERSONAL RELATIONSHIPS WITH OTHERS

EASY CAP PATTERN

Hail Mary full of grace, the Lord is with you.
Blessed are you among women and blessed is the
fruit of thy womb, Jesus. Holy Mary, mother of
God, pray for all sinners, now and at the hour of
our death. Amen

For teen and adult caps: J, K, M, or N sized hook. 4 ply yarn.
For infant and child caps: F or J sized hook. Baby yarn.

Crown
Chain three. Connect them in a circle. Chain two. Every time you end a row, you're going to do a slip stitch and two chains.

For the base row, put five single crochets inside the circle. Slip stitch (slip stitch means you slide the hook behind the chain-two below and grab a loop and pull it through everything on your hook). Now chain two.

For the first row, put two single crochet stitches through both loops in every stitch all the way around. Slip stitch (slide the hook behind the chain-two below and grab a loop and pull it through everything on your hook). Now chain two.

The second row, put one single crochet through both loops of the first stitch and then two single crochets through the next stitch and repeat that all the way around. One, two - five times. Slip stitch and chain two.

The next row is one single crochet twice and then two single crochets once all the way around. Pattern: One, one, two – five times.

The next row just adds another single crochet to the pattern: one single crochet three times and then two single crochets.
Pattern: One, one, one, two – five times.

Then one single crochet four times and two single crochets.
Pattern: One, one, one, one, two – five times.

Then one single crochet five times and two single crochets.
Pattern: One, one, one, one, one, two – five times.

The last row of the crown is one single crochet in each stitch all the way around. Now your crown is complete.

Body of the cap
Next eighteen to twenty-four rows (your choice): The body of the cap is worked as a single crochet in each stitch, but done in the back loops. End each row with a slip stitch and chain two.

Brim
Next three rows: Double-half-crochet in both loops all the way around. End each row with a slip stitch and chain two.

For the last row, turn and single crochet through both loops all around, slip stitch and tie off. Weave the remnant yarn through the 2 chain spots.

Crochet has a rhythm to it that lends itself to scriptures, prayers and sayings. Once the crown of the cap is complete, I say the rosary along with the stitching. I'm not Catholic, but I love the rhythm and graceful words. I see nothing wrong in asking you to pray for me. In the same way, I see nothing wrong in asking Mary to pray for me. Along with the Ave Maria lines, you can repeat the Gloria Patri, the Lord's Prayer, the Apostle's Creed, and the Doxology.

Feel free to sew on flowers or bobbles. You can work these caps in solids or multicolored yarns. Stripes are fun – change the yarn at the chain-two spots. If you are keeping one color throughout the stripes, don't tie it off, just keep it waiting at the chain-2 spot until you can pick it back up again. You can also work this pattern with two threads at the same time for a much thicker cap.

Video on how to make caps for charity:

https://youtu.be/hrkf9kz7Jfs

HOW TO UNWIND A SKEIN

Matthew 22: 37-40
Jesus replied: "'Love the Lord your God with all
your heart and with all your soul and with all your
mind.' This is the first and greatest commandment.
And the second is like it: 'Love your neighbor as
yourself'. All the Law and the Prophets hang on
these two commandments."

I watched with concern as a friend struggled with her yarn.
Her stitches were well-shaped, her shawls always looked beautiful,
and her borders enhanced the overall flow of the pattern. But she
struggled with the yarn. It would fray and she jabbed her hook
through it rather than under it. Pulling yarn through the loops, she
would catch a few of the fibers below. Her shoulders were tense,
her expression severe. She was not enjoying herself.

We talked about what might be the problem. She walked me
through everything – nothing was wrong. And then I glanced at her
skein. She was unwinding the yarn from the outside.

(You can uncover your eyes now, that's the worst part of this
horror story!)

I don't ever remember reading this first and foremost rule of
using yarn: *Thou shalt unwind the skein from within*. I think it ought
to be stamped on every skein sleeve, like the warnings of impending
death on cigarette packages. Some skeins show little pictures of the
two directions you can pull the yarn: from around the outside and
from the center. There are no written explanations on this, but I
think the caption under the *from the outside* picture should be
NEVER DO THIS.

The fibers which become yarn are twined in one direction. Honest. Go unravel a piece of yarn and try to twist it the other way. It won't work. But twist it back in the direction the machines twined it, and it will become whole again. As you knit or crochet, you should continue working in the direction the yarn was originally twined.

Sometimes, it is difficult to find the end piece hidden inside the skein. Be diligent; pluck out a whole bunch of yarn and gently unravel it until you find the beginning. You will be amazed how easily the rest of your work flows from this one commandment: Begin at the center.

In life, I can do wonderful things that look beautiful, are useful and appreciated and praised. But if I do not have the first commandment at the center of my life (Love the Lord my God with all my heart, soul, and mind) then everything I do will be difficult and unfulfilling. Once I began loving God with everything within me, the second commandment (love my neighbor) flows easily and fills me with grace, joy, and hope.

My God, fill me with your presence. Break my heart. Engulf my soul. Consume my thoughts. Let me be totally Yours. Nothing I do will have any meaning if You are not the center of my being. Amen

Your personal notes:

TO CROCHET OR TO KNIT

To Knitters -- ***Proverbs 19: 14***
Houses and wealth are inherited from parents, but a prudent wife is from the Lord.
To Crocheters -- ***I Corinthians 7: 8***
Now to the unmarried and the widows I say: it is good for them to stay unmarried, as I am.

A knitted shawl is soft, feminine, and brings comfort to the wearer. A crocheted shawl does exactly the same thing.

Booties protect and warm the feet of babies whether they were knitted or crocheted.

Crocheted afghans serve the same purpose as knitted ones.

I have never read a commandment anywhere that states, *Thou shall knit.* Or *Blessed are the crotcheters even though they only have half the hooks as knitters.*

There are some patterns and some yarns that lend themselves better to crochet than to knit. And definitely, there are some people who are better suited to knit than to crochet.

But the purpose of both is to create and the end result is the same.

I know how to knit; I just never caught on to knitting as well as I did to crocheting. As a crochet artist, I invent my own patterns, teach others, and produce projects well. As a knitter, I lost count, dropped stitches, forgot which direction I was going, and usually produced a miserable looking scarf (which the pattern described as a king-sized afghan.)

I believe God created me to crochet. If, eventually, God wants me to knit, He will provide evenly matched needles and a pattern well suited to my talents and His ambitions. (It sure would be nice if God gave me someone who loves to sing.)

In your shawl ministries, try to include knitters and crocheters. Some work well in pairs; others work best singly. But if God is the Master Designer, the end results will be the same.

Jesus, never let me forget to include every woman into my circle of friends. Don't ever let me expect someone to spend time with me and exclude their spouse. Don't ever let me offer an invitation in such a way that a woman would not feel comfortable attending if she came alone. To some people, you gave the gift of holy matrimony. To other people, you gave the gift of being unmarried. You chose the gift for us, not the other way around. Don't let me forget that. Amen.

Your personal notes:

VALUE

Romans 8:28
And we know that in all things God works for the good of those who love him, who have been called according to his purpose.

My favorite shawl pattern calls for fifteen ounces of four-ply yarn. The material costs about eight dollars and I can complete one in eight hours. Another pattern calls for forty-four ounces of two-ply yarn for about thirty-two dollars and takes at least a week to make because the directions are so intricate. Both patterns result in gorgeous shawls of the same dimensions which are received equally well. The materials cost different amounts of money and time, but the true value is how the materials are used.

Christian works are very much like shawls. Some projects cost more than others in material, time, and attention to detail. But the end result for all Christian works should be the same -- leading all souls to heaven.

I can't sing in front of thousands -- well, I could, but the thousands wouldn't appreciate it. I can't physically build a house or adopt orphaned refugees. I have very little medical skills and speak only English and a grocery-store-smattering of Spanish. But I can crochet. And I can pray. I pray over the things I crochet and pray for the people who receive the things I crochet. And praying helps lead people to Jesus. And whoever believes in Jesus will have everlasting life.

Salvation is the most valuable gift in the world.

My Savior, help me accept the limitations to my talents, not by being discouraged or by giving up, but by using what I can do to further your kingdom. Whatever I can do, let me do it so that all souls will be led to heaven. In your name I pray, Amen

Your personal notes:

ACCEPTING GRACIOUSLY

1 Thessalonians 5:16 – 18
*Be joyful always; pray continually; give thanks in
all circumstances, for this is God's will for you in
Christ Jesus.*

Thank you.

These are two simple words that stumble across women's lips and mysteriously unlock a tiny drawer, or a closet, or a massive warehouse of doubt and insecurities.

In response to a compliment, women say, "Thank you, it's so old."

In response to a present, women say, "Thank you. You shouldn't have."

In response to praise, women say, "Thank you, but I didn't really deserve this."

Is it any wonder why people shy away from giving compliments to women?

Years ago, I learned a secret about receiving gifts (praise, compliments, et cetera). The giver is pleased when I just accept graciously. Thank you, said with honest gratitude, is sufficient. The gift is validated and the giver feels appreciated.

I thank God the same way I do a friend. His gifts are overwhelming and magnificent, and I do not deserve them, but I thank Him for them every day. I don't gush insincerities, nor do I negate His gifts by pointing out my unworthiness. I thank Him, because I love Him.

Sweet heavenly Father,
Thank you.
Amen.

Your personal notes:

CONFIDENTIAL CHARITY

Luke 17: 2-3
It would be better for him if a millstone were hung around his neck and he were cast into the sea than that he should cause one of these little ones to sin. ³ Pay attention to yourselves! If your brother sins, rebuke him, and if he repents, forgive him.

Most of my life has been spent as an elementary teacher. As a result, I have this face that seems to be respected and trusted by total strangers. The fact that it also breaks cameras is fine. I'll take trust and respect over photogenic allure any day. I also hate to stand in lines, so I talk to people. I love talking to people, and inevitably, someone bares their soul to me.

What a blessing to me, that God uses me to help open the doors to people's hearts.

My Prayer Shawl Ministry members collect cards during the two weeks between our meetings. These cards have the name, prayer requests and delivery instructions for those who would benefit from receiving our shawls. There are times when *too much information* is shared on a card or discussed in a meeting. There is a line between what we need to know in order to pray, and what really is none of our business. Obviously, some of the difficulties these recipients go through are sensitive in nature -- or the fodder of juicy gossip!

These recipients are going through the worst of times. They are also putting their trust in Christian women by sharing their hurts and prayer requests. They are as vulnerable as children during this time. And you know what Jesus said about hurting a child.

As a teacher, I have found myself longing to see millstones

miraculously appear around some parents' necks. I will never forget the belt buckle scars embedded in my student's skin, the burn marks down their tiny arms, the jagged slashes down their legs from thorny switches. I will never forget their hot tears and sorrowful sobs. These children were victims of betrayed confidence.

Be sure, as Prayer Shawl Ministry members and leaders, that you never betray confidences. Treat all prayer requests as confidential.

Jesus, let your will be done in each woman's life. Let me treat her with respect and keep her confidences. Let me be to her as You have been to me: a counselor, a comforter, a friend. Amen.

Your personal notes:

BABY BOOTIES

__Luke 18:16__
But Jesus called to him, saying, "Let the children
come to me, and do not hinder them, for to such
belongs the kingdom of God."

During the autumn of 2004, my small town was crossed by the paths of four hurricanes. My house was without electricity about one out of every three weeks during that time. Schools were cancelled, roads were blocked. So I crocheted. I developed this pattern by experimentation, and when the fourth hurricane had seen the last of my small town that October, I had bags filled with over ninety pairs of booties and about three dozen baby blankets. A year later, I gave them to the Teen Parent Center (one of my many schools that year). I was delighted that these things which were created in such a time of despair were used to celebrate times of birth.

Booties are worked in two parts: the foot and the cuff. They can be worked in any size yarn, but the smaller the hook, the smaller the bootie. Baby yarn and size f or smaller hook makes a new-born size. Four-ply yarn and size f hook makes a one-year size. In general, one skein with seven ounces of yarn will make nine pairs.

Foot:
- chain 3, join in circle
- Turning chain (chain 3, turn – called the 'turning chain' here and throughout), 17 DC in circle
- Ruffle: Turning chain, using front loop for ruffle: (sc, chain 3 sc, chain 3) in each loop for 3 stitches. Then sc, chain 3, sc in the next stitch.
- SC in back loop of next stitch. In back loop of each individual stitch here and throughout:
  - SC
  - hdc two times
  - DC two times
  - 2 DC in next 2 stitches
  - DC two times

- o hdc two times
- o SC two times. (This should put you at the ruffle.)
- 12 chain. Attach with slip stitch at the other side of the ruffle (where you ended the last chain and began stitching around the medallion).
- SC in each stitch around medallion. DC in each chain stitch
- Next row: SC, Decrease by one SC in two loops. (sc, decrease 2sc) Repeat to end of row.
- Next row: Decrease by one SC in two loops to end of row. (dec2sc)
- Next row: Decrease by one SC in three loops (dec3sc three times.) Tie off. Pull knot and yarn into the foot and weave and trim.

Cuff:

- Attach with slip stitch directly behind first stitch of ruffle. SC, Decrease by one SC in two loops. Repeat until you get to other side of the ruffle. SC in the back (front to you now) loop of each ruffle. Slip stitch to close.
- Turning chain. Begin working on the outside of bootie. DC in each stitch. Use the inside loops behind the ruffle to complete the ankle as a circle. Slip stitch to close.
- Turning chain. DC in each stitch. Slip stitch to close.
- Turning chain. DC behind each DC column of previous row. Last DC should be worked behind the turning chains of this and the previous row – you will have to fold down the cuff.
- Slip stitch to base of second row. Tie off and pull yarn inside bootie. Weave and trim

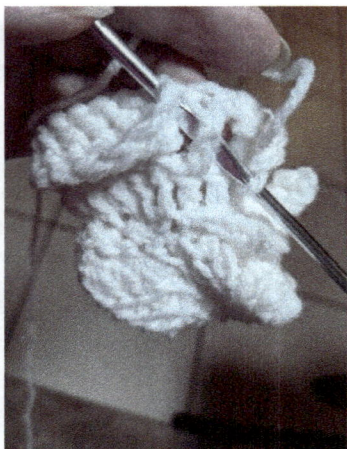

Make 2 for each pair . . .

WHO IS IN CONTROL?

Psalm 40: 4
Blessed is the man who makes the Lord his trust,
who does not look to the proud, to those who turn
aside to false gods.

I facilitate writer's groups. I ran my Prayer Shawl Ministry. I sing soprano in my choir. I drive my car. I own my house. I am a woman in charge of my life.

In every situation, there will always be someone else who tries to take over my meetings. There will always be some piece of equipment or material which will diminish my control over my environment. Men may have *good old boy* systems, but women have *pecking orders*. There always seems to be someone trying to peck their way to the top and trample me on the way.

This used to bother me immensely. I would cry. I would get angry. I would say vindictive things and instigate sweet revenge. I was miserable. I was tolerably successful but absolutely miserable.

So what happened? I learned to trust God. I put Him in control.

Now I tell my writers groups that I am the facilitator, not the dictator, and we all share an equal part in the group. I take a more pro-active role in my Prayer Shawl Ministry as an organizer, but we are equal participants. In my educational career, I stopped putting myself in charge of my peers and now enjoy just doing my job. I blend my voice with the choir and it sounds so much better than a bunch of soloists singing at the same time.

I am a woman in charge of my life. I'm in charge of my life because God is in control of me. I defer all major decisions to Him.

I discuss all situations with Him. He is my counselor. He unfolds the universe at my feet and shows me where to step. (I don't always follow the path He shows me, but I admit that He was right when I eventually wind my way back.) He never leaves me. He never forces His decisions on me; I have free will. I choose to have God be in charge of my life.

That's the secret of a successful Prayer Shawl Ministry. You run it, but let God be in control.

Dearest God,
Remember when I said You could guide me and
guard me? Remember when I asked you to protect
and preserve me? And about that whole direct and
defend me thing – please do. Always. Forever. Be
in control of my life. Thank you! Amen.

Your personal notes:

HOW TO DEAL WITH THEFT

Matthew 18:21-22

21 Then Peter came to Jesus and asked, "Lord, how many times shall I forgive my brother or sister who sins against me? Up to seven times?"
22 Jesus answered, "I tell you, not seven times, but seventy-seven times."

I made a preliminary count of the caps we were going to send to Avon Park Youth Academy. It was only June and these would be the boys' Christmas presents, but I wanted to see how far we were and how much more we needed to do. We had about 125 caps and needed 165! I was so pleased. I packed the caps back away in our cabinet and told the PS ladies they could slack off on the caps and spend more time on shawls or baby things – whatever they wanted.

In one of our regular meetings that November, we were ready to begin wrapping the caps in the cute brown sacks we'd bought so I could deliver them when I went to the academy in December. Counting the caps we brought in from over the summer, we only had 35 caps.

I immediately contacted our minister. Yes, the room was locked, but most of the church's members had a key, plus we had custodians and bug spray people and I'd never given it a thought.

We knew that these caps were sometimes the only present the boys would get. We couldn't let them down. With heroic effort, my prayer shawl ladies worked for three weeks nonstop and made up the difference. People from all over heard of what had happened. A week before Christmas, I cheerfully delivered 165 caps to our boys, plus we had a dozen more left over for next year.

The locks were changed. I was given one key; the other was kept in the office. Workpeople were now let into the room by the secretary and we kept the room clean ourselves.

The following year, I kept the caps in a huge zippered plastic case and marked the caps on a sheet as I gathered them every meeting from the women who brought them. We only needed 120 this year. By June, we had 125. By October, we had only 35 again. The plastic case was empty and had been shoved behind some afghans on the bottom shelf of the cabinet. The sheet with my tallies was still there.

Some things that had disappeared a year ago reappeared. But things we had in plain sight tended to disappear when we least expected it. The five totes full of yarn suddenly would have only a few old skeins. I'd arranged them by colors per tote; the skeins would be rearranged different ways the next time we'd meet.

Baby things began to disappear from the cabinet and shawls walked away from the drawers.

The second meeting that October, I sent all of our shawls to Friends of the Fallen. All of them.

My minister put a padlock on the cabinet. I have the only key.

We delivered 120 caps to our boys the first week of December.

I sell things on eBay and teach classes on how to do so. Caps of the kind we make sell for between $8 and $45 on line. Each theft of caps gained someone over a thousand dollars – a felony if convicted.   I strongly believe that people should face the consequences of their actions. Over and over I have asked myself, "Do I press charges against one of my sisters in Christ, knowing she would face years in prison?"

Over four hundred people are wearing prayed-over caps we made for our boys. Did it matter that the recipients weren't in jail themselves? Did it matter that someone profited by our hard work and the money we spent for the yarn and the time we took to make the caps?

I prayed for God to take care of the situation the first time it happened. And everything worked out well. I nearly quit the Prayer Shawl (and the church) when the second theft was discovered. I prayed even more this time that bitterness and suspicion would not ruin our group. You see, it had to be someone who had access to the office and knew where things were in the prayer shawl room. And on top of that, it had to be someone who brought things back, too.

What was actually stolen? Our talent? Our gifts? Our time together? Our prayers for the recipients of the caps and baby items – no matter who they might be? No. Only the items were taken.

Had we let it, these thefts could have destroyed us.

As it turned out, the thefts made us stronger and more productive. They bound us together and whoever it is who took the caps knows that we keep him/her in our prayers. How sad to be that person – to know that these simple caps could mean so much more than mere money – to know that we forgive her/him and pity her/him. I believe who ever this person is needs our love and prayers. And isn't that the reason we join together as a prayer shawl ministry – to pray for each other through times of distress and trouble?

We did, however, keep all the caps we made during the following year at our own homes until packing day in November.

Sweet Jesus,
Help us to remember that all things pass away.
Only love remains. Forgiveness is ours for the
asking, and ours to give, too. Let us realize what
our true treasures are and that these treasures can
never be taken away.
Amen.

Your personal notes:

CELEBRATE AS FRIENDS, TOO

Deuteronomy 8:10
*And you shall eat and be full, and you shall bless
the Lord your God for the good land He has given
you.*

I always believed that dinner was the time for family members to come together and share the events of their days over well-cooked meals and laughter.

As a child, my parents rarely excluded us from the table – special events where we had to sit at smaller side tables were the exception. As a parent myself, I diligently tried to set aside dinner for my son and I to spend time together. As a solitary adult, I find that dinner consists of all vegetables or snacks that can be eaten while I'm working on my computer. Friends of mine who are married tell me that most of the dinner time is spent being attentive to their spouse's needs.

What dinner should be isn't actually what it is for most women. If you were to take a poll of the women in your prayer shawl circle, I would imagine dinner is more work than nurture for them.

Your prayer shawl meetings are filled with a lot of conversation while your fingers work. So even though there is fellowship, the main activity during your meetings is work.

Find a time about once every three months for your prayer shawl circle to meet at a restaurant and eat a good, wholesome meal. The restaurant should have waiters and soft music. During dinner, your ladies should relax, enjoy, eat, and talk. Don't work all the time. Learn to become friends, not just at work, but during peaceful times, too.

One of my favorite meals with my prayer shawl circle was our trip to a Chinese restaurant in Winter Haven. I was really surprised to discover that most of them had never been to a Chinese restaurant before. I rediscovered my favorite foods by helping them decide what was tasty and daring and what should best be left alone! At the end of the meal, we all read aloud our fortunes from the cookies. We learned more about each other that day than we had in the six months that we had been working together.

There are some unspoken parameters which need to be addressed before you decide on a place to eat:

- ✓ How much does it cost? Can all of your members afford it without too much sacrifice? Get a copy of the menu before making a final decision. The price range should be such that someone could order a full meal or salad bar comfortably.

- ✓ When are you going to meet? If the timing excludes someone because she works or has a special responsibility at that time, change the time. Brunch Saturday morning to be followed by an expedition to a local yarn shop can be a lot of fun. You might try to have a luncheon after church (and invite your non-church members to attend as your guests). Early evening get-togethers can accommodate those who work in your town so they don't have to go all the way home and then turn right around and drive back. If it's during the night, make sure all attendees have a ride – many women don't like to drive alone after dark; some women have night blindness.

- ✓ Take into consideration any special dietary or physical needs. Rule out any restaurants which would exclude your members. Special dietary needs could also include weight-consciousness as well as alcohol awareness. Make sure there is a place for your crocheter in the wheelchair and your knitter who can't gracefully climb up on those tall stools.

✓ Make sure someone has already eaten there. I'll take personal experience over a newspaper ad any day!

✓ Call the manager and discuss how many you plan to bring. Ask if you need to make reservations, if there is a special place you all can be seated, and if there is a set gratuity for that number of guests.

✓ If you enjoyed the meal, write a thank you note to the manager and attach a flyer or business card for your prayer shawl group. They will most likely post your card and information where other guests can see it. What a wonderful way to advertise your ministry!

My Dearest Friend,
Be with us as we visit and share a good
meal. Let us always be grateful for this
wonderful place you have brought us to.
Help us find friendships that will support
and defend us and last our lifetime.
Amen.

Your personal notes:

SEASONS OF MEMBERSHIP

Ecclesiastes 3:6
A time to seek and a time to lose,
A time to keep and a time to cast away

People will join your group because they hope it will meet one of their needs. Once those needs have been met, they either stay because they now belong to a group from which they cannot imagine leaving OR they leave because they got what they wanted from the group and are going elsewhere in search of solving other needs. Sometimes they leave because they never found whatever it was they were seeking.

This is normal. The ebb and flow of membership may seem like an undertow of betrayals and insufficiencies to a leader who is insecure. But to a woman who understands that "there is a season for everything," these tides of membership will not sweep her away.

Create a place of warmth and welcome. Understand that it is not your role in the universe to make someone else happy, nor is it to solve all the problems of other people. Accept whoever walks into the door. Keep in touch with (but don't guilt) the people who leave.

And preserve and protect the sisterhood of all who stay.

Father,
I will do my best to maintain a place of safety,
respect, and purpose in the prayer shawl room.
Send us those who need us. Send us those we need.
If we are not the group for them, let them find
sanctuary some place.
Amen.

Your personal notes:

DIFFERENT PRODUCTION RATES

Luke 21:1-4
Jesus looked up and saw the rich putting their gifts into the offering box, and he saw a poor widow put in two small copper coins. And he said, "Truly, I tell you, this poor widow has put in more than all of them. For they all contributed out of their abundance, but she out of her poverty put in all she had to live on.

I am a very fast crocheter. We have had women in out ministry who are incredibly productive. We also have women who work diligently for a month or two on a simple cap.
Every stitch is precious. Every item completed is a gift. Every pair of hands that works for the good of the world is blessed.

As your members bring in their items, make a concerted effort not to praise the quantity more than you praise the effort.

I know we could not have met our goals of shawls, caps and afghans if it had not been for some women who were prolific crafters. But just as honestly, we could not have met our goals of shawls, caps and afghans if it had not been for the women who could only make one thing.

Don't forget to praise often, praise deeply, and appreciate all gifts and all givers.

Bountiful Lord Jesus,
Thank you for the gifts you give us. Thank you for
the talents you teach us. Thank you for seeing the
two tiny copper coins we each can give. Thank you!
                    Amen

Your personal notes:

FABULOUS FLOWERS

"Would that the lovely flowers were born to live
Conscious of half the pleasures that they give."
~~ anonymous needle work

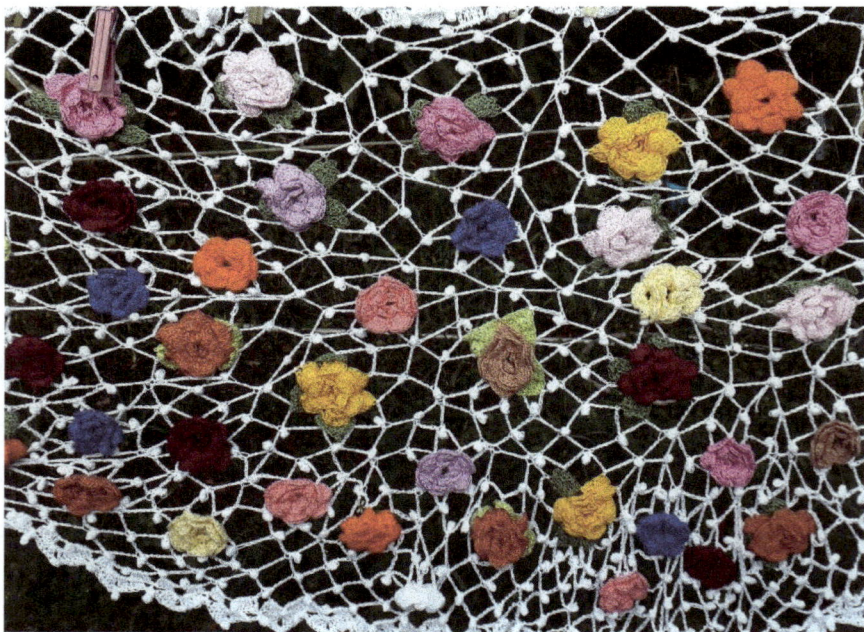

Flowers add such a lovely touch to hand-crafted items. And they are so easy; you will be tempted to crochet entire bouquets to adorn your work!

Centers
Width:
Sc for small center, DC for larger center

Chain 4, join in circle.
Large: Chain 3, 17 DC in circle. Slip stitch to first chain 3.
Small: Chain 2, 17 sc in circle. Slip stitch to first chain 2.
Tie off if you're going to use another color for the petals or
continue if the same.

Various textures:
- Popcorn stitches for large center (like sunflower)
- Sc, ch 1 or 2, sc – makes a frilly center
- Work stitches on the front loop makes a harder center (cone flower or poppy)
- Crochet beads into the centers for a sparkly effect.
- Yarn content makes all the difference!!

Petals
Basic:
(Sc, chain a certain number, sc) repeated around the center stitches
i.e. (sc, chain 3, sc) in same stitch. Work each petal around the
center

Numbers:
Each petal is worked in one stitch of the center. Use the back loop
of the center if you want the petals to appear to grow behind the
center (like a rose), the front loop if you want the petals to seem to
come out from the center (like a poppy), or through both loops to
make the center appear plump (like a daisy).   You can skip a loop

or do petals in the front loops in one row and then the back loops in the next row – depends on how many petals you want.

Shaped:
Use a series of symmetrical stitches for each petal, complexity determines size and thickness of the petal. The stitches range in increments as such: slip stitch, sc, hdc, dc, tr
Examples:
- Sc, hdc, dc, tr, dc, hdc, sc makes a nice rose petal
- Sc, sc, dc, dc, tr, tr, tr, dc, dc, sc, sc makes the top petal of a violet
- Sc, dc, dc, sc makes a simple clover petal

Don't be afraid to try various shapes for each flower, no two petals are exactly the same!

Elongated:
Chain the number of stitches to meet your length requirements. Turn. (Divide the number of chains by 3. Work that many (N) of each of the stitches, one per loop, as follows.) In next N stitch(es), sc. Hdc in next N stitches. Dc in next N stitches. Slip stitch to adjoining loop on flowers center. Repeat around center for as many petals as you wish. Note: elongated petals do not have to be all the same length!
For example:
Slip stitch onto back loop of a center. * Chain 12. Turn. In second stitch from hook, sc. Work one stitch in each loop as follows: sc, sc, sc, hdc, hdc, hdc, hdc, dc, dc, dc, dc. Slip stitch to back loop of next stitch of center. Repeat from * around the center.

Leaves

The initial chain determines the length of the leaf. The complexity of the stitches along the spine or in the circle determines the shape/width of the leaf.

Short, plump: (work stitches inside the circle formed by the chain) Chain 4, join into a circle. Chain 2, 1 sc in ring, 2 hdc in ring, 1 dc in ring, 2 tr in ring, chain 3. 2 tr in ring, 1 dc in ring, 2 hdc in ring, 1 sc in ring, ch 2, sl st in ring. Pull tight.

Elongated: (work stitches along the chain – first one side, then the other)
Chain 10. Turn. Sl st, sc, hdc, 2 dc, sc, 2 sl st to end of leaf. Turn. Working in top loop only: sl st, sc, hdc, 2 dc, sc, 2 sl st to end. Fasten off.
Change the number of each stitch to form the shape you want.

Attaching it to something else

You can easily attach something to a flower or attach the flower to a larger piece by sewing or crocheting it.

You can also use the flower as a center of a granny square or circle. You have to build a framework behind the center of the flower with a simple slip stitch and chain for each side of the framework. If you want to make it into the center of a square or circle, you will need four corners (the slip stitches) and four chains of equal length. You could make a three-sided framework if you were going to make a circle or a triangle. Just change the number of sides to suit your needs.

Working on backside of flower, make a chained square:
Slip stitch on back loop anywhere on center. Chain (3 for small, increasing to no more than 5 for larger centers), slip stitch at 90

degree angle from first stitch. Chain (3 for small, increasing to no more than 5 for larger centers), slip stitch at 90 degree angle from second stitch (which will be 180 degrees across from first stitch). Chain (3 for small, increasing to no more than 5 for larger centers), slip stitch at 90 degree angle from third stitch (directly across from second stitch). Chain (3 for small, increasing to no more than 5 for larger centers), slip stitch onto first stitch.

Attach the leaf/leaves to the slip stitch on the back of the flower center just before you make an attachment chain.

You can tie off or turn and begin working with flower facing you. Use the chain-spaces to work whatever you wish to make. Granny squares are the same as circles, just with corners. So you would 3Dc through one chain space, chain 2; 3 dc in the next chain space, chain 2; 3 dc in the third chain space, chain 2; 3 dc in the last chain space, chain 2. Slip stitch to first stitch and continue the square as you would any other granny square pattern. If you wanted to make the flower into the center of a circle, repeat the above directions, but leave out the chain 2's for the corners.

Vary the number of slip-stitch-chains to create triangles, pentagons, whatever you need. Use only one chain space across the back of the flower if you wish to incorporate it into a row.

Dear Maker of all,
Sometimes it takes just a little extra effort to change
a plain afghan into an extraordinary one. Lives are
like that, too.
Thank you for the flowers you scatter along the
roadsides and push up along the cracks in the path
ahead.
Amen

Irish Rose	https://youtu.be/YjREbF4qicY
rose part a	https://youtu.be/xBbsqkC4pRg
rose part b	https://youtu.be/-juZSnkNx4c
leaves to rose	https://youtu.be/Wuu3lK8Z-Zg

PRAYER

Matthew 6: 9 – 13
"This, then, is how you should pray, 'Our Father in heaven, hallowed be your name, your kingdom come, your will be done on earth as it is in heaven. Give us today our daily bread. Forgive us our debts, as we also have forgiven our debtors. And lead us not into temptation, but deliver us from the evil one.'"

Luke 11: 2 – 4
He said to them, "When you pray, say: 'Father, hallowed be your name, your kingdom come. Give us each day our daily bread. Forgive us our sins, for we also forgive everyone who sins against us. And lead us not into temptation."

Every night before I go to sleep, I begin my prayers, "Dear God, let your will be done in my son's life. Let us be a family again." People who follow Jesus don't have perfect lives or perfect families. Don't expect a life of bliss and domestic tranquility; it's not going to happen. Jesus doesn't smooth the road ahead; He becomes the light that guides our feet.

Jesus taught us how to pray. Two examples are listed above. This is the pattern for the perfect prayer. I strongly encourage you to study the Lord's Prayer. Don't worry about the whole sinners versus debtors versus trespassers thing. Those are just words.

Comprehend the concepts:
- o God is holy.
- o The fulfillment of God's will completes the master design for the universe.
- o Trust that God will meet your needs.
- o Ask God to forgive your sins.
- o Forgive people.
- o Believe that God will not leave you during times of trouble.
- o Praise God.

I used to worry that I was wasting God's time. After all, He was dealing with war, famine, pestilence, starving children, and terrorism, not to mention volcanic eruptions and hurricanes. I just had a very quiet, mundane, small-town life.

I slipped into the habit of praying for others. When I hear an ambulance I pray, "Lord, guard and guide." When I see a policeman or a helmet-less biker, I pray, "God, protect and preserve." When I see a child, I pray, "Sweet Jesus, direct and defend." It's very simple; very easy. It doesn't take a lot of time out of my busy schedule. Plus, it gives me the feeling that I am praying without ceasing.

At night, in my pajamas and my nice comfortable bed, I ask God to help specific people in trouble. I name them all and tell God about their problems.

For years, this was how I communicated with God. It was like I was constantly forwarding e-mails to God without telling him about me: my needs, my troubles, my hopes, my joy. I closed my prayers the way I close my e-mails, "Love you! Evelyn."

I was a very busy prayer-er, but I ignored the fact that I was important to God. He loves me. He doesn't just want to hear **from** me; He wants to speak **with** me.

I learned the hard way that I can't save anyone. I learned the hard way that the only person I can control is myself. I learned the hard way that I am not in charge of the universe. Most importantly, I learned the hard way that God loves me.

I stopped forwarding prayers to God and began begging, "God, help me. I need you."

This shift in relationship has changed my life. I still pray for those I see around me. I still lift the cares and burdens of friends up to God. I always pray that God's will be done in my son's life. But I talk to God now.

That's what prayer is meant to be; not just sending communications to the Divine God, but having conversations with my Sweet Lord.

To me, prayer is the most important part of this Prayer Shawl Ministry. We are not just a group of people making handmade clothing. We're not just a group of people giving away clothing. We pray. This defines us. This empowers us.

As you pray over the shawls and for the recipients, don't forget to talk to God. Ask Him to guide you and to guard you. Ask Him to protect and preserve you. Ask Him to direct and defend you. You are important to Him. He is omnipotent, omnipresent, omniscient, and extremely busy. But He will always take time to listen to you.

Pray.

[Insert your prayer here.]

GLORIOUS GRANNIES

Romans 5:3-4
The people of God rejoice not only in future glory but in present trials and sufferings, not because trials are pleasant but because they produce a step-by-step transformation that makes believers more like Christ.

There must be hundreds of books of granny square patterns (I myself have half a dozen!) Once you understand the intrinsic quality of a granny square, you can design your own. And they don't even have to be square!

Basic beginning:
Chain 3, join in circle

First row:
Chain two (counts as launch stitch = one double crochet)
2 DC inside circle
Chain
3 DC inside circle
(one **corner** made)

Repeat number of corners you want for the shape
Triangle: 3 corners
Square: 4 corners
Pentagon: 5 corners*
Hexagon: 6 corners*
Heptagon: 7 corners * (good luck fitting these together!)
Octagon: 8 corners*
* These shapes require a "basic beginning" circle made from a 5 chain.

Slip stitch into first launch stitch to end each row

Second row:
Chain two (counts as launch stitch = one double crochet) plus one more chain
Skip the first part of the first corner and work in the chain stitch:
3 DC inside chain stitch
Chain
3 DC inside chain stitch

(one **corner** made)

Chain, 3 DC in space between the corner sets, chain

Work the shape by putting the **corners** in the chain stitch between the **corner halves** and putting chain, 3DC, chain in the spaces between the corners (sides).

Last side: 2 DC, slip stitch into 2 chain (launch stitch of that row)

Consecutive rows:
Continue putting chain, 3 DC, chain in side spaces and **3 DC, chain, 3 DC** in each **corner**.

Change colors at launch stitch.

Rectangles
Beginning: Chain 5, join into circle

First row:
Chain two (counts as launch stitch = one double crochet)
2 DC inside circle
Chain
3 DC inside circle
(one **corner** made)
Chain, 3 DC in circle, Chain (one side)
3 DC, chain, 3 DC (second corner)
Chain
3 DC, chain, 3 DC (third corner)
Chain, 3 DC in circle, Chain (third side)
3 DC, chain, 3 DC (fourth corner)
Slip stitch to launch stitch of that row.

Repeat rows: **corners into corners**, <u>sides into spaces between sides</u>.

Sets

- To make the 3 DC more triangular, do not put a chain between the sets
- To make the 3 DC more square, PUT a chain or two between the sets
- 3DC sets can be replaced by popcorn stitches, shell stitches, ruffles, etc, as long as the basic pattern is followed.

To change a circle into a square

Remember – Balance is the Key.

Determine where the corners will go and use Triple Crochet for those stitches. Use DC in the first sets on either side of the corners. Decrease the size of each set, HDC on either side of the DC sets. Decrease again if there are more sets: single crochet. Slip stitch if absolutely necessary for any remaining sets (these will be in the middle of the sides).

If your circle is 36 stitches around:

*(Tc, chain 2, tc) in both loops of first stitch. One of each in the following stitches: Dc, hdc, sc, sl st, sl sti, sc, hdc, dc. Repeat from * 3 more times. Sl st to first TC.

Next row: sc in back loops along sides, (2 sc, chain 3, 2 sc) in each corner chain space. This will give your new square a less floppy appearance.

Joining the shapes

- **Border**: Back sides together, SC through both sides' back loop.
- **Invisible**: Right sides together, SC through both sides' front loop.

- **Lacy**: Back sides together, work one shape and then go to the corresponding stitch on the other shape: SC, chain, SC, chain. Repeat for each stitch pair. Shape A and Shape B such that:

SC on A, chain;, SC on B opposite A

SC on B next to first B, chain, SC on A opposite the second B

Continue pattern A, chain, B; B, chain, A; A, chain, B; B, chain, A; A, chain, B; B, chain, A…

- **Ridge**: Use the Border directions above, but place a chain between each SC

Using Colors

- Change colors at launch stitch.
- Use the same number of colors as you have corners or as many colors as you have rows.
- Use solids with blending variations.
- Use hues of equal intensities (all pastels or all neons or all traditional, etc.)

Yarns

Beginner and Intermediate crocheter – use the same weight of yarn and size of hook throughout.

Highly advanced crocheter – mix and mingle various threads, materials, weights, and hook sizes.

Binding

To bind them into a larger piece, use the same color you want to come out as your main color (i.e. the one you used for the inner circles or the one you used the least, or the one you used the most), or use a contrasting color (black, white, brown).

Border

To border the piece, try scallops, lacy chains, or fringe, etc., whichever fits your finished product.

My Master,
Teach us your lessons. And then teach us your
lessons again and again. We are slow to recognize
your wisdom and often reluctant to follow the step-
by-step directions which would lead us along the
path you have for our lives. Teach us again and
again until we recognize the pattern of your plans.
Then help us to teach it to others.
Amen.

Your personal notes:

Granny Rectangle https://youtu.be/MKMatMnOLqA

Granny Triangles https://youtu.be/1l59hKSGoQk

MINISTERIAL RELATIONSHIP WITH THE WORLD

CHOOSING & ENCOURAGING REPLACEMENT LEADERS

Matthew 10:16

*Behold, I am sending you out as sheep in the midst
of wolves, so be wise as serpents and innocent as
doves.*

The prayer shawl ministry should not be dependent on you; it should be based on the circle of members and the plans God has for them. As such, you need to choose a potential replacement leader. It bares thinking about. It really bares praying about.

I laugh and tell my groups that I am a facilitator, not a dictator. They laugh in return and sometimes roll their eyes or give each other knowing looks. But I know there are going to be times when I just can't make the meetings. And eventually, there will come a time when I will be in Heaven and the group will have to go on without me.

If I were gone tomorrow, I hope my ministry would go on because it is based on the circle of women and God's plans. But I need to begin now to prepare and encourage other women to take leadership roles in the group.

Every January, our first meeting is set aside to plan out what we want for the coming year. We discuss missions and recipient groups and mini-lessons as well as times of fun and fellowship. This is a good time to also coax women to take on other responsibilities of the group – a secretary, a treasurer, a postal runner. You might also – if your group is large enough – divide the items into groups and set up someone to be responsible for them – the shawls could be organized by one woman, the baby things could be itemized and organized by someone else, etc.

It is very difficult to be the sole person responsible for every aspect of a prayer shawl ministry. Not only do people grow to expect you to run everything, you begin to believe you actually can and should run everything. Share the responsibilities.

And when it comes time for you to leave, you will have prepared many willing and capable leaders to step in and take your place. Your ministry will continue, as will God's plan for it.

Our Father,
We are sisters in your house. We share the joys and
sorrows equally. Help us to share the
responsibilities, too. Help us to knit ourselves
together and like a multi-colored granny square, let
us all be different in our own special ways, but let
us be one in purpose.
Amen

Your personal notes:

TEACHING OTHERS

Matthew 28: 18-20
Then Jesus came to them and said, "All authority in heaven and on earth has been given to me. Therefore go and make disciples of all nations, baptizing them in the name of the Father and of the Son and of the Holy Spirit, and teaching them to obey everything I have commanded you. And surely I am with you always, to the very end of the age."

I learned to crochet when I was about eight or nine. I was fascinated by it. I also learned to knit at the same age. I learned by watching someone do this.

Over the multiple decades since then, I have been called upon many times to teach someone to crochet or knit. There are books, videos, and DVDs that proclaim easy ways to learn these arts. However, the best way to learn is to watch a friend – stitch by stitch -- who has become experienced in the art.

I sit the learner beside me on my right. I twist a brand-new piece of yarn around my hook and laugh with the learner who has never seen that particular knot before. And then we begin.

"Relax your hands. Don't strangle the hook. Let the yarn flow, but keep a slight tension on it. Your left hand holds the material and guides your hook into the right spot." All this is said before the first chain.

"Lower your shoulders, take a deep breath. Relax. No, no, release the death grip you have on that hook!"

And we laugh again.

Slowly, I show how to loop the hook under the yarn and swirl around and draw it through with my right hand while I pull down on the stitch between my left thumb and middle finger and adjust the tension on the yarn slipping between my left pinky and ring finger.

"One chain! Good job!"

Eventually, we get a long series of chains and begin the meticulous process of single crochets, advancing to double crochets, and turning the piece properly.

We laugh a lot. We also learn how to deal with knotted yarn, dropped stitches, strangled spaces, and tying off and on new colors.

Teaching others about Jesus is very similar to teaching crochet. You must have patience, endurance, and laughter. You must be willing to teach someone how to deal with mistakes and unfamiliar situations. You must encourage your students to follow directions and trust the pattern of life. There are many books, songs, DVDs, and videos on how to live a Christian life. But the best way to learn it is from watching a friend.

Be that friend.

Dear Lord,
Put me in a place where I can teach others about
You. Help me keep living a Godly life so I know
what I'm talking about and so when others watch
me, what they learn from me will be the right things.
I want to show people the difference You have made
in my life. I need to lead others to You. Let me be
that friend. Amen.

Your personal notes:

EMBELLISHMENTS

John 7: 24
"Stop judging by mere appearances, and make a
right judgment."

I love jangly-dangling earrings. I also love bright swirly skirts and swoopy-cowl-necked sweaters. And shoes – oh my gracious -- how I love fun shoes!

My mother says not everyone can wear the things that I do. What she probably means is that no one would dare wear them. That's okay -- she's right.

When I choose a shawl for myself, I go for the flowers, shells, sequins, and tiny bells. I am not wild about fringe. The most beautiful shawl I ever made was for my mother -- metallic gray, tiny stitches, with lots of mesh; no embellishments. Mom hates embellishments. Shawls are shawls though, and both of these shawls served the same purpose.

Be careful what embellishments you add to a shawl. Shawls should reflect the recipient's personality. The embellishments don't change the use of this shawl, but they can detract from the shawl's usefulness. I would love spangly-danglies on the shawl and would wear it. My mother would thank me graciously for a spangly-dangly shawl, and hide it forever in the back of the linen closet.

My faith has a lot of spangly-danglies attached to it: powerful prayers, enlivening songs, joyful tithes and offerings. But it is not the spangly-danglies that are important; it is the faith itself. I don't expect anyone to wear my faith, nor do I allow anyone to foist their faith on me. Faith is faith. The importance of faith is not how it looks to others, but how it is used.

*My Lord, my Savior, my Beginning and my End,
I want to praise you every single moment of my life
and keep praising You on the other side of
mortality! I want to dance and sing and laugh with
You. I want You to wrap me in your arms and hold
me as I sob. I want to be solemn and honor the
sanctity of your presence, too. Don't let me distract
others from worshiping you by my enthusiasm.
Don't ever let me judge someone who keeps silent
nor someone who makes a spectacle of themselves
while praising you. Keep my faith strong. Amen.*

Your personal notes:

CARRYING BAG

1 Samuel 16:7
But the Lord said to Samuel, "Do not consider his
appearance or his height, for I have rejected him.
The Lord does not look at the things man looks at.
Man looks at the outward appearance, but the Lord
looks at the heart."

I found it in a thrift shop, stuffed in a box filled with worn backpacks and old purses. It looks like it might have at one time been a chair cushion, and someone put a strap and an embroidered flap on it. The embroidery is of Tudor roses and was obviously once part of a larger tapestry. The zipper opens into a cavity large enough for a double-sized skein, a half-finished shawl, and several crochet hooks. It has a front zippered pocket below the Velcro patch large enough for a small pair of scissors and half a dozen Prayer Shawl Ministry brochures. It cost about three dollars.

I carry it with me at all times. It is a wonderful conversation piece. It carries the tools I need, and I can hand out brochures for those who show interest.

Women in my Prayer Shawl Ministry also have found ways to carry the things they need for this ministry. One uses a plastic grocery bag. Another carries little plastic boxes for her tools. Earth-friendly shopping bags are also popular. It doesn't matter what the carrying bag looks like, its worth is inside.

I'm short, plump, and middle-aged, with an honest face and an easy laugh. Depending on my purpose for the day, I may wear a suit with heels and hose or jeans, T, and sandals. God gave me the brains of a genius and the body of an old maid school marm. It doesn't matter what I look like on the outside. What matters is what I hold inside. I have the materials to work and share within me at all times: scriptures, personal experience, faith, songs, joy, hope, and love of Jesus.

> *Lord, don't let me come up wanting in the ways that would help others find You. Fill me with your love. Keep me learning your word. Sing songs within my heart that I can share with others. If I get a little thread-bare along the way, that's OK. Let me always treasure the things inside my heart and mind and soul. Allow me to see that in others, too. Amen.*

Your personal notes:

WHY HOOKS AREN'T MADE OF GOLD

Proverbs 8:17-19
I love those who love me, and those who seek me
find me. With me are riches and honor, enduring
wealth and prosperity. My fruit is better than fine
gold; what I yield surpasses choice silver.

Wars have been won and lost over it. Murders have been committed for it. Marriages are banded in it. Prizes are named after it. Gold: civilization's most precious metal.

Anthropologists claim that the first age of tools were wooden implements. Wood is common, easy to shape, easy to replace, and from a renewable resource. The first needles and hooks were wooden.

Most of the hooks in my bag are aluminum or plastic. These materials are renewable, common, sturdy, and inexpensive. I've never had one break or bend -- when used properly -- and have given dozens away. I can easily find them at stores, thrift shops, and garage sales. I never worry about them being stolen.

I was surprised to learn how soft gold is. It is described as a malleable metal. It's not strong. It does not tarnish or corrode like other metals. Gold is often the target of thieves, and it is very expensive.

Crochet hooks or knitting needles would not work well made of gold. They would be very pretty, but they would bend from use. I couldn't afford many of them, and certainly would be reluctant to give them away. As I sat in the waiting rooms crocheting, it would be the hook not the shawl which attracted bystanders. When offered a hook and a skein, the stranger would snatch them, but not to learn how to crochet; not to become a productive giver.

The emphasis of any project should not be on the tool, but the end result.

I am content to be common, sturdy, and reliable. I don't want people admiring me. I want them to benefit from what I do.

Father, keep me common and unremarkable. Allow me to be used for your kingdom, power, and glory, now and forever. Amen.

Your personal notes:

BASIC RIPPLE BLANKET

Proverbs 17:6
*Grandchildren are the crown of the aged, and the
glory of children is their fathers.*

One of the first things I ever identified as crocheted was a ripple afghan my father's mother gave us when I was four. It was all sorts of autumnal colors, and its pattern fascinated me. The ripple pattern can be adapted in so many ways: the length of the rises and falls, the stitch itself – or combinations of stitches, the thickness and the color of the yarn, the size of the hook. You can make each ripple afghan different with no two the same for years. There is no elaborate pattern one must follow, so it is the perfect project to sit in church or in front of the TV or in a waiting room and do.

Simple, yes, but there are secrets which must be adhered to in order to come out with a straight-edged, rectangular afghan.

A ripple consists of one rise and one fall. We'll call each rise and each fall **B** because they are the same length.

Each afghan has a certain number of the rise/fall **pairs**. We'll call those pairs **C**. For most afghans, 6 works well as C.

To gage the correct number of stitches to chain at the first, you multiply **2B with C** which we will call **A**.

Infant ripples are made using size F hooks with a thickness of 3. Child ripples are size J hook with a thickness of 4. Both infant and child ripples are 7 stitches in the rise and 7 in the fall. Adult ripples are made using size J and thickness of 4 but have 9 stitches in the rise and 9 in the fall.

So infant/child ripples are 2 times 7 times 6 = 84 = A

Adult ripples are 2 times 9 times 6 = 108 = A

The beginning chain for any ripple is (2 times B times C) plus 1 or **A plus 1**. Infant/child = 85, adult – 109.

Row one has a different valley number. In all the rest of the rows, you skip 2 stitches at the valley. But in the first row, you only skip one stitch.

For all rows, the mountain has (stitch, chain 2, stitch) in the previous chain space. The first stitch counts as the last stitch of rising B. The chain 2 is where each mountain top will be put. The next stitch counts as the first stitch of the falling B. So, the basic pattern looks like this: **(B-1), (stitch, chain 2, stitch), (B-1), skip 2 stitches.**

Examples: infant afghan is 6, (stitch, chain 2, stitch), 6, skip 2. Adult is 8, (stitch, chain 2, stitch), 8, skip 2.

Now, the secret to this project lies in how you do the first rise and the last fall of each row.

Secret 1: the first rise

For the second and following rows, you will chain 2 or 3 (depending on your stitch – 2 for sc, hdc; 3 for dc or tc), turn, and **skip the next stitch**, then crochet B-2 and then the last stitch of B in the chain space.

Chain 2or 3, skip one, (5 or 7) stitches, (stitch, chain 2, stitch to begin the next fall).

Secret 2: the last fall

Crochet the (stitch which is the last of the previous rise, chain 2, stitch to begin the last fall) in the mountain top. Then crochet B-2 stitches. You will place the last stitch between the columns of the last and second to last stitches of the previous row. Not through the loops, through the columns.

(Stitch which is the last of the previous rise, chain 2, stitch to begin the last fall), (5 or 7) stitches, one stitch between the last columns. Chain 2 or 3, turn.

It is through these first and last stitches that you will crochet your border.

RIPPLE AFGHAN PATTERN

Chain A plus 1

Row 1:

- First rise and fall: skip 2 chains and begin first stitch in the third from the hook. A-1 stitches. Chain 2, 1 stitch in the same chain. A-1 stitches. Skip 1 stitch.
- Second rise and fall: A stitches. Chain 2, 1 stitch in the same chain. A-1 stitches. Skip 1 stitch.

- Third rise and fall: A stitches. Chain 2, 1 stitch in the same chain. A-1 stitches. Skip 1 stitch.
- Fourth rise and fall: A stitches. Chain 2, 1 stitch in the same chain. A-1 stitches. Skip 1 stitch.
- Fifth rise and fall: A stitches. Chain 2, 1 stitch in the same chain. A-1 stitches. Skip 1 stitch.
- Sixth (last) rise and fall: A stitches. Chain 2, 1 stitch in the same chain. A-2 stitches. Gather all remaining chain loops onto your hooks and crochet one stitch through them. Chain 2 or 3. Turn.

Row 2:

- First rise and fall: skip 2 stitches and begin first stitch in the third loop. A-1 stitches. Chain 2, 1 stitch in the same chain. A-1 stitches. Skip 2 stitches.
- Second rise and fall: A stitches. Chain 2, 1 stitch in the same chain. A-1 stitches. Skip 2 stitches.
- Third rise and fall: A stitches. Chain 2, 1 stitch in the same chain. A-1 stitches. Skip 2 stitches.
- Fourth rise and fall: A stitches. Chain 2, 1 stitch in the same chain. A-1 stitches. Skip 2 stitches.
- Fifth rise and fall: A stitches. Chain 2, 1 stitch in the same chain. A-1 stitches. Skip 2 stitches.
- Sixth (last) rise and fall: A stitches. Chain 2, 1 stitch in the same chain. A-2 stitches. Skip 1 stitch. Place last stitch

between the columns of the previous row. Chain 2 or 3. Turn.

- Row 3- however many you want to make it the length you desire: Repeat row 2.

Borders:

Frame your project by using hdc stitches for the first row of the border: Down the sides, place 2 hdc stitches in each column if the stitches were hdc, 3 if dc, 4 if tc. Across the top, place one hdc stitch in each of the previous row's stitches, (stitch, chain 2, stitch) in the chain spaces, skip 2 in each valley.

Put three in each of the four corners.

Second row of the border: Down the sides: (sc, hdc, dc, tc, picot, tc, dc, hdc, sc) as a repeat – one in each stitch – through both loops. Across the top, place one stitch in each of the previous row's stitches. (hdc, picot, hdc) in the chain space of the peak of the row below. Skip 2 in each valley. Put three in each of the four corners. Slip stitch to close. Weave in.

Note: picot is chain 3, sc stitch in third from hook. Advanced crocheters may use Clones knot instead of a picot.

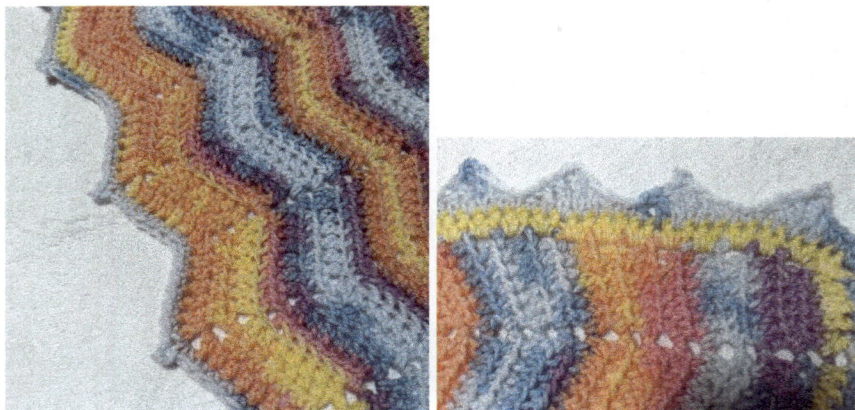

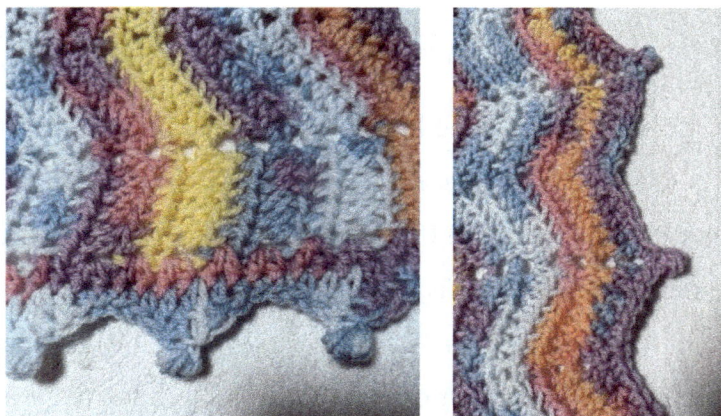

My sweet Lord,
As this blanket is wrapped around an infant, wrap him
or her also in your love, protection, and grace. Now and
forever, amen.

Your personal notes:

OPPORTUNITIES

Matthew 7:7-8
*"Ask and it will be given to you; seek and you will
find; knock and the door will be opened to you. For
everyone who asks receives; he who seeks finds;
and to him who knocks, the door will be opened."*

I carry my crochet bag with me everywhere I go. I crochet
while watching TV, while visiting with friends, while waiting for
appointments, and while being driven places (not while I myself am
driving). People watch my fingers in fascination and we begin to
talk.

I tell them what I'm making and let them feel the material. I
tell them about the Prayer Shawl Ministry and the Teen Parent
Centers and the Prayer Shawls for Fallen Soldiers' Families. Then
I offer them an extra crochet hook and a spare ball of yarn and ask
them if they would like to learn.

What a wonderful way to open doors! By telling them about
what I'm doing, I help revive the dying art of crochet. By letting
them feel the project, I make a connection between concept and
reality. Touching the material also links the stranger to good
childhood memories of beloved mothers and grandmothers who
crocheted or knitted. By telling them about the Prayer Shawl
Ministry, the Teen Parent Centers and the Prayer Shawls for Fallen
Soldiers' Families, I open two doors: one of participation by way of
membership or donations, the other of possible new recipients of
prayers and shawls. Finally, by handing them the tools, I offer them
an opportunity to begin a new journey.

I take my Master with me everywhere I go, too. I live my religion, opening opportunities for people to ask me questions and reconnect with Jesus. I talk about my beliefs, opening opportunities for participation and receiving prayer. I share my faith, offering prayer, scripture, and songs as tools to help others begin a new journey to salvation.

Master, don't let me skip over an opportunity to share your kindness with strangers. Don't let me be too busy to comfort a friend. Don't let me be too tired to listen to the needs of my family. When someone knocks, let me be the one You allow to open the door. Amen

Your personal notes:

BEGINNINGS AND ENDINGS

Ecclesiastes 7:8
The end of a matter is better than its beginning, and
patience is better than pride.

I have a bed covering that I absolutely love but it is not usable. I began each medallion with a colorful flower and centered each flower inside a white triangle. I then arranged the triangles in circles and bound them with green stitches like leaves. However, I miscalculated either the number of flowers or the geometry of the triangles, so I filled in some areas with white patches. The border had to be elaborate, so I ruffled pink and rose to match the flowers, and then ribbed light and dark green for the leaves, and of course I had to add another frilly edge of white. I have a queen-size bed. The bed coverlet swallowed the bed and dragged along the floor for several feet.

I was having so much fun with the pattern, I didn't know when to stop.

Sometimes, I get so tired of the color or the pattern I'm doing, I quit working on it before it is finished. I hope those people who received child-size shawls and twin bed-size afghans will forgive me; I just didn't want to keep going.

Beginning a project is so much more exciting than finishing one. But there is nothing useful about an unfinished shawl or an incorrectly sized afghan.

Sometimes, we need to just stop. We need to know when something -- even a good thing -- is over. Don't waste time longing for something that's done. Think about the joy of beginning something new. You only have one pair of hands. You can't work on two projects at the same time. End one so you can begin anew.

My God,
You know how stubborn I am. You know how
engrossed I can become in something. Help me to
understand that it is time to go on to something
new. Don't let me fear new beginnings. Don't let
me fear endings, either. I have all of eternity ahead
of me. Teach me to let go and go on. Amen.

Your personal notes:

HANGING YOUR WASH ON THE LINE

John 15: 1-4
"I am the true vine, and my Father is the gardener.
He cuts off every branch in me that bears no fruit,
while every branch that does bear fruit He prunes
so that it will be even more fruitful. You are
already clean because of the word I have spoken to
you. Remain in me, and I will remain in you. No
branch can bear fruit by itself; it must remain in the
vine. Neither can you bear fruit unless you remain
in me."

One year, I made a decision to be more productive but less busy. I had filled my life up with *busy* and found myself not completing many of my plans. Plus, I was forty-seven years old!

So I started hanging my clothes out to dry. Yes, you read that correctly. Instead of dashing into my laundry room to toss a soggy load of clothes into my dryer, pushing a button, and dashing away to the next project, I took the clothes outside and hung them on the line.

I love being outdoors, but I never seemed to take time to go outside. I was so busy I couldn't find the time to think. So I started hanging my clothes out and discovered some wonderful things. I love being outside again, and my clothes smell of the outdoors even when I put them away. Hanging up clothes gives me the time to think simple thoughts and to ponder large mysteries. Plus, I realize how the previous week has gone. I first realized this when I glanced out my kitchen window, wondering if the wash was dry, and saw a field of red. Almost everything on the line was red. I had been fighting several battles that week; I guess I had dressed accordingly. The next week--disaster after disaster--the clothes pinned to my lines were black, gray, and brown.

I made a concerted effort to vary my hues. If my emotions influence my color choice, perhaps the opposite would work, too. This morning, I hung out florals, stripes, and solids in every color. It had been a terrible week, but I don't think any but my closest friends noticed, and I feel wonderful today.

At the beginning of every prayer shawl meeting, I write in a ledger the name and prayer need for each shawl recipient. This book stays with me and is not for public display. But, like clothes on the line, it shows me what needs are being acknowledged by my group. It also shows me when there are glaring gaps in some areas. If one week is full of widows and the next is full of grieving daughters, we have done a good job comforting those who mourn, but what of the others? The abused woman in the shelter? The cancer patient? The woman whose career is in jeopardy?

A mentally healthy week is reflected by various colors on my clothes line. A spiritually healthy ministry is reflected by the varied needs which are being met.

O Gardener of my soul,
I don't want to be so busy that I stop being
productive. In my productivity, let me be well-
rounded. Let me be a vine which bears fruit that
meets the many different needs of those around me.
When You prune me, let me accept the need for rest
and restoration, so that I can bear fruit again.
Amen.

Your personal notes:

HOARDING SUPPLIES

Matthew 6: 19-21
*"Do not store up for yourselves treasures on earth,
where moth and rust destroy, and where thieves
break in and steal. But store up for yourselves
treasures in heaven where moth and rust do not
destroy, and where thieves do not break in and
steal. For where your treasure is, there your heart
will be also.*

My Prayer Shawl Ministry has Yarn Angels who spend their Saturday mornings -- and their money -- gleaning boxes of yarn from garage sales. Along with the brand-new and used skeins of yarn are half finished projects: baby blankets, dozens of tiny granny squares, armless sweaters and sweater-less arms. It's so sad.

My spare bedroom is packed full of bags of yarn and unfinished projects and pattern books. One whole drawer is filled with crocheted flowers. I work diligently to turn every skein of yarn into something useful. I scold myself when I buy yarn for a new project when I have so many skeins already. But I buy it anyway.

It's so sad.

Yarn is unfulfilled potential when it is in a spare room or set aside for a rainy day.

I have put an addendum in my will -- all yarn, hooks, needles, and craft books will be given to my Prayer Shawl Ministry at my death. I like that idea, but I would rather give away completed shawls during my lifetime.

Sometimes I wonder what spiritual resources I am hoarding. Did I refrain from sharing a smile because I myself was grumpy?

Did I forget to pray for someone because I was too wrapped up in something else? Did I wear out my voice hollering when I should have been singing? And comfort, did I save it for loved ones and deny strangers?

When I go to heaven, I hope to leave behind finished projects, not unused supplies.

*Jesus, let me be generous with the things
You give me. Love, hope, joy, understanding,
compassion, wisdom, faith: help me share these
things. Help me use these things to further your
kingdom. In your name I pray. Amen.*

Your personal notes:

LEAD ALL SOULS TO HEAVEN

John 3:16
*"For God so loved the world that He gave His one
and only Son, that whoever believes in Him shall
not perish but have eternal life."*

I'm not sure what kind of bird it was--I'm not really up on my bird identification skills. It was smaller than my palm, with a narrow beak, a stripe of yellow below its eyes, and a swab of red above its breast. Smaller than a robin, larger than a sparrow; it hopped along the top of my curtain rod in my living room.

I wondered how in the world it got in. Then I wondered how it was going to get out. I turned off the ceiling fan and watched as it hopped from my curtain rods to my cabinet and then to the slowed blades of the fan.

I opened the top window in my front door and went back into the living room. I think it was attracted by that hint of fresh air. The bird flew past me, through the front hall, and into my study. By now it had the undivided attention of Moonbeam and Daisy. Moonbeam --I tossed into my bedroom and shut the door. Daisy, adorable Lab that she is, quickly lost interest.

I wanted to rescue this bird and set him free. I turned off the ceiling fan in my study and watched as the tiny bird explored the room. If I swooped on him, he would panic. If I tried to capture him, he might be injured. I tried warbling to him, but I'm not very good at bird-talk.

I retreated into the living room. The March breeze from the hallway window was strong enough to be felt in the study. It attracted the bird. He flew into the hall and perched on the wicker shelves filled with African violet pots. I closed the door to the study and stood in the doorway to the living room, effectively blocking those two exits. Slowly, calmly, the bird explored the pots on the wicker shelves. It was two feet away from the open window. If I startled it now, it might fly away from the opening, and I would have accomplished nothing.

The wind gusted into the house, promising a month that would go out like a lamb. The bird flew toward me, pin-wheeled, and soared out the window. I cheered, Daisy barked, and Moonbeam got let out of the bedroom: the bird was free.

Sometimes, the urge to help people find salvation is so great; I have to hold myself back. I want to shout, "This way!" I want to swoop down and drag them toward salvation. Sometimes, I hope they can be scared into finding salvation.

None of these strategies should ever be employed by prayer shawl ministries. The best way to help someone find salvation is to remove what might endanger them, make the way to salvation obvious, and remove any obstacles in the way. Gradually help the person recognize spiritual dead ends. And pray, "Lord, let your will be done in this person's life."

I believe I have the responsibility to open the window. The bird was the only one who could fly through. The wind blows. The bird recognizes its true environment. The bird finds his way home.

Lord, let your will be done. Amen.

Your personal notes:

TAM O'SHANTER OR RASTA CAP
FROM GRANNY SQUARE

Romans 12:9
Let love be genuine. Abhor what is evil; hold fast to
what is good.

If you are like me, you have a bag of really incredible granny squares that you loved making but then got bored with before you'd made enough to make anything with them. I have some terrific books on dozens and even hundreds of granny square patterns. Some are even triangular!

A few summers ago, I vowed to make four of each type of granny square in a certain pattern book. I learned a lot of interesting stitches and created some fascinating squares. By the end of the month, I had a laundry bag full of squares 12 by 12 and 18 by 18. A few were 9 by 9, and there was to occasional 6 by 8. They were in coordinating colors of purple, gold, brown, olive, and black. (Harry Potter was popular that year). I learned a lot by making the squares, but I lost inspiration for making anything from the squares.

The next October, when we discovered we must make a hundred caps in less than 2 months, I glanced at the bag of caps and wondered, "What if..."

To make a square into a circle is easy – arch the stitches along the straight sides by increasing the degree of your stitches and then decreasing them (sc, hdc, dc, tc, tc, dc, hdc, sc) and slip stitch on the corners.

Then I needed to decrease the overall number of stitches around the circumference of the new circle to about 35 (the normal number of stitches in the simple cap pattern).

This done, I had what resembled a beret. So I crocheted a few more rows as a brim and voila! It didn't look French; so I dubbed it a tam O'shanter. Siobhan! Made with a larger opening, a thicker brim, and wider granny squares, these make wonderful rasta caps!

Materials:
A nine inch square or larger
Yarn of coordinating color
J - N size crochet hook (depending on yarn thickness)

Row 1
Join coordinating color yarn into any corner with a slip stitch, chain 1. SC in each stitch and one in each chain space, sc-chain 1-sc in each corner. Slip stitch into initial chain 1.

Count the number of stitches to the next corner. Divide that number by 2 and then that number by 4. This is the number of each kind of stitch you will make between the corners (in pattern below, this number is represented by the letter N and remainders by the letter R).

For example, if there are 36 stitches along the side, 36 divided by 2 = 18. 18 divided by 4 is 4 with 2 left over. Use the remainders as the number of slips stitches on each end of the pattern. N=4, R=2 (Slip stitches are worked through both loops. Stitches are worked one in each of the back loops of stitches below.)

R Slip stitch
N sc
N hdc
Ndc
N tc
N tc
N dc
N hdc
N sc
R slip stitch.
Repeat for each side.
Join with slip stitch to first stitch, chain 2.

Row 2
SC in back loop all around.
Join with slip stitch in the chain 2 space. Chain 2.

Row 3
*2N-1 sc (one in each stitch); 1 sc in two stitches – both loops
(reduce). For example, if N is 4, then 2N-1 = 7.
Repeat from * all around.
Join with slip stitch in the chain 2 space. Chain 2.

Sequential rows
Measure around your forehead just above the ears.
Repeat row 3 until you have **that many inches** around the
circumference of your circle. Begin counting at 1 at the beginning
of each of these rows, no matter what number you ended with
before the slip stitch and chain 2.

Next 2 rows
Hdc in both loops around. Join with slip stitch in the chain 2 space.
Chain 1.

Last row
Turn. Sc in both loops around (2N-1 stitches and then combine
two stitches into one). Join with slip stitch in the chain 1 space.
Finish off.

Sweet Maker of All,
Help us to remember that we have the ability to
change. We can change squares to circles and
circles to squares. We can change lives and hearts
and futures. Sometimes it takes time. Sometimes it
comes about through dire need. Let us never feel
stuck with what we have. Let us use what You have
given us to meet the needs of others. In your name I
pray, amen.

Your personal notes:

A PIECE OF YARN

Matthew 18: 18-20
"I tell you the truth, whatever you bind on earth
will be bound in heaven, and whatever you loose on
earth will be loosed in heaven. Again, I tell you
that if two of you on earth agree about anything you
ask for, it will be done for you by my Father in
heaven. For where two or three come together in
my name, there I am with them."

One piece of yarn can be useful: tie something together, measure something, attach one thing to another. Okay, so it's not incredibly versatile, but it is nice to have around.

I am like a piece of yarn.

Take this same piece of yarn and weave that into a simple square. Now it is stronger and much more useful.

I am like this simple square when I join with friends for a simple purpose.

A piece of yarn, woven by a master, can become an afghan, a sweater, baby booties, a kitchen potholder, or a delicate doily. The yarn is still yarn. The design determines the yarn's usefulness and strength and value.

I am this same piece of yarn when I surrender to the Master's design for my life.

Sweet Jesus, weave me into the lives of others. I surrender to your will for my life. Join the people in our group together, so that what we do in your name will magnify You on earth and in heaven. Bind us into one fabric. Take this one single life and knit it into the lives of others to become a useful ministry. Now and always, Lord, Amen.

Your personal notes:

SENDING TO OTHER COUNTRIES

John 16:33
*I have said these things to you that in me you may
have peace. In the world, you will have
tribulations. But take heart; I have overcome the
world.*

What could be more exciting than sending hand-crafted items to children in foreign lands? I used to dream about being a (young, beautiful and single) missionary in an exotic place (with young, handsome and single pastors assisting me). As I matured beyond Christian Romance fantasies, I realized that I was still yearning to help children far away.

Children everywhere are in need of food, clothing, shelter, and a nurturing environment. As a prayer shawl ministry, we have more than enough clothing we can share.

Certain governments, however, take a different view.

McLeod Prayer Shawl Ministry is on Facebook. We have friends. I don't post as often as I should, but I still meet people from all over the world who are interested in our ministry. One such man was a minister in one of the most deprived areas in the world in Nairobi, Kenya. He was always so vibrant and evangelical that I kept tabs on him, occasionally commenting on his posts, and he on mine. He helps run a home for children and women and they were without so many things. I asked how we could help.

In January 2012, I presented the idea to my ladies and between us, we packed a huge copier-paper-size box full of children's items – caps, blankets, layettes, booties, and toys.

I researched how to send things to another country. I began with the United States Postal Service's website. I read over their "prepare international shipments" section. I also read over *eBay's Policies on Embargoed Goods and Prohibited Countries* section. At the time of this writing, we as an American group cannot send anything to these embargoed countries:

- Burma (Myanmar)
- Cuba
- Iran
- North Korea
- Sudan
- Syria

I went further afield for more information: eBay's *International Shipping and Customs* page which led me back to the USPS's page on *Postal Explorer > International Mailing > Individual Country Listings*. Click on any country to read what you may and may not send to that country.

There are size and value limits for each country, too. There is also a link to any customs forms that you must fill out. Some have to be typed, others handwritten. You need to know the exact contents of the box and the weight and dimensions of it. An approximate value as well as a purpose need to be written on each form where required. And ALL of the necessary forms need to be filled out before you head to the post office.

Rev. Mulwa was in Kenya. We had caps and other hand-crafted items to send him. However, Kenya prohibits "used clothing, bedding and other similar items, textile and fabrics" from other countries. Not to be daunted, I filled out the custom pages and had help from my local Post Office to do so. These weren't used items; they were brand new! So we called them Humanitarian Aid items and for $50, I shipped a box worth about $100 to Kenya and the orphans there.

A week later, I'd heard nothing. Two weeks later, I'd heard

nothing. A month later, I got a message from Rev. Mulwa that the box had arrived, but there was what amounted to $150 of customs charges due. I went back to my PO and was assured that everything was paid for and I did not owe anything, but "some countries do things differently."

I explained to Rev. Mulwa that we were not able to pay such an amount. He was extremely disappointed and we left it at that.

October 2012, I received a badly beaten but still unopened box back from Kenya. There was no explanation on the box as to why it had been returned.

So take your time and do research and explore the USPS's page   on   Individual   Country   Listings http://pe.usps.com/text/imm/ab_toc.htm

Jesus said to go unto every nation preaching his gospel. The US Customs service has other ideas. Do what you can with the countries you can. And pray for God to send someone knocking on your door.

Jesus,
I will not get aggravated by the tribulations and red
tape of this world. I will rejoice in the fact that you
have overcome the world, and that your will is
going to be done.
Amen.

Your personal notes:

BUGS & VARMINTS

Joel 1:4
What the cutting locust left,
The swarming locust has eaten.
What the swarming locust left,
The hopping locust has eaten.
And what the hopping locust left,
The destroying locust has eaten.

Any time you store something, you will have unwanted guests. Critters by nature are always in search of food and shelter; hand-crafted items often provide both.

More than this, you have to protect your work from mold, mildew, dust and animal dander.

There are many ways to keep your hand-crafted items free from bugs and varmints. However, the use of pesticides and other chemicals needs to be excluded from this list as much as possible. Your shawls, lap quilts, afghans and baby items will often be given to people who are ill or who have weakened immune systems. Chemicals exasperate these conditions.

Cleanliness is next to Godliness – you've heard this as a child. The first step to keeping your hand-crafts critter free is to keep your ministry room clean. Look for signs of droppings, unusual piles of dust, and webs. Sweep, mop and then spray the perimeter of your room.

Set up a way to package the items while you wait for them to be distributed. We use plastic bags, zippered bags left over from buying sheets and comforters, and plastic containers and drawers. Plastic keeps moisture in, so make sure the items are dry before sealing the bag. Some plastics can smell, too. Take a whiff of the bags – if they smell, keep them opened until the smell dissipates or put a small scented soap bar in with the items. Clear bags that have a white label are great – you can write a description on the label to keep from having to open the bags each meeting.

Toss a bay leaf into each bag (remove it before giving the item away). Bay leaves – as you all know – keep weevils and moth eggs at "bay" (forgive the pun).

Animal dander and dust can easily be removed by a short spin in the dryer under the air cycle. Toss in a scent-free dryer sheet to cut down on static cling.

Machine wash any items that you receive from a thrift store or garage sale. If a member or someone in their household smokes, politely set up rules about the quality of the items they make – wash it before bringing it to the meeting.

A last word, scents are nice and pleasant but a little bit goes a long way. Mothballs and cedar are long lasting and seem to grow in intensity over time. Don't use them inside the bags. Don't let them touch the yarn. Never use musk, it is highly allergenic and ages poorly. Florals are sweet if used lightly. If it makes someone's nose itch, don't use it! Never spray the fabric directly. If the item smells badly, it should really be washed and dried before being given away.

Dear Creator,
You made all the creatures on the earth and I'm
sure you had good reason to create each and every
one of them. Help us keep them out of our stuff,
though. OK, Lord?
Amen.

Your personal notes:

FINANCES – THE COST OF GIVING

Philippians 4:19
*And my God will supply every need of yours
according to his riches in glory in Christ Jesus.*

So how much does it cost to run a prayer shawl ministry?

Other than the obvious yarn and hooks or needles, you will need to have plastic bags, manila envelopes, tissue paper, cards, gift bags, business cards, stamps, tape, pens, totes and drawers, as well as books and patterns.

How many of each of these you will need depends of course on how many items you give away.

Bags, tissue paper, cards, pens and envelopes can be found at thrift shops and dollar-type stores. Totes and drawers can be found at garage sales and discount stores for less than twenty-five dollars. Plastic bags and manila envelopes can be bought in bulk at warehouse-type stores. Tape can be bought in bulk at office stores or on sale right after Christmas.

The money for stamps can be donated through your church or host organization. Generally, I can mail a shawl anywhere in the United States for about nine dollars. Ironically enough, I can pack six prayer shawls into a copier-paper-size box (the one that holds 10 reams of paper) and mail it to Dover for almost the same price as one shawl in an envelope. The mailing envelopes and boxes that cost a flat fee are nice – you can budget your postage if you consistently use these.

Business cards. Business cards are a must for a vibrant ministry. They are small and easily carried in bulk. Keep them close at hand so that when someone comments on your crochet or knitting, hand them a card as you explain the ministry. You can hand them two cards at a time and ask them to keep one and pass one on. You can print them yourself using a computer document program and store-bought cardstock. You can order them from local office stores. There are several high-quality on-line businesses which offer the first 500 cards for free. On it, have your ministry's name, a purpose statement, and contact information – phone, email, etc. We tuck a business card inside the cards we include in the gift bags and envelopes. We also include a card in the giftbags our church gives to visitors.

Brochures are a nice way to advertise your ministry. You can develop several of them on any word document – including various backgrounds and colors. They do cost a lot to print on nice paper stock, though, so use them sparingly.

Generally, most people provide their own crochet hooks and knitting needles. They are very personal items. I've found many knitting needles at thrift stores and strangely enough, very few crochet hooks. There is a bag full of them in our ministry room so that anyone can have them if they need them.

Yarn is also very personal. One lady loves bouclé and crochets with it well. Another lady works miracles with homespun yarn. I love variegated acrylic. We use what we like, so we usually buy our own yarn, too. However, you may want to develop a yarn kitty for your ladies to draw from.

Overall, the most expensive part of a prayer shawl ministry is postage. Ask your minister if you can have five minutes of the church time and pitch an appeal for postage donations.

We've been giving away shawls, caps, baby items and afghans for years and we've never run out of money, supplies, or talents. Trust and God will provide.

Heavenly Provider,
Show us how and we'll do it. Provide for what we
can't pay for. As long as we are doing your will, I
know it will get done.
Amen

Your personal notes:

BEST WAYS TO SHIP

Philippians 1:6
And I am sure of this, that he who began a good
work in you will bring it to completion at the day of
Jesus Christ.

You need to protect your hand-crafted items along the journey to their recipient. The journey will be fraught with water (rain, moisture), gravity (squished and pummeled), sharp edges (sort of sums that up as is), and other dangers such long journeys hold.

Step one: Pray over the item.

Step two: Wrap the item in lovely tissue paper. Have your ladies sign an appropriate card. Put a business card or brochure inside the card. Tuck the card inside the tissue paper, too.

Step three: Place the wrapped item inside a tight-fitting plastic bag. If you can't do this, use clear plastic wrap and tape the item so that no tissue or fabric is exposed.

Step four: Place the plastic-wrapped item inside a larger manila envelope or cardboard box. Cushion around it with newspaper or brown sacks (but be careful of the ink of the newsprint).

Step five: Put an index card with the recipient's address on it inside the box, taped to the plastic.

Step six: Seal the box or envelop with clear plastic shipping tape.

(Masking or duct would work, but it might look a tad tacky...)

Step seven: Address the box with the recipient's and your ministry's mailing addresses. Print this information in the appropriate spots. Cover both spots with clear plastic tape. (Ink smears if it gets moist.)

Step eight: Take the package to your post office or mailing business. Ask for the cheapest rate. If there is only a dollar or two difference between the cheapest and next higher rate, go with the better rate. For 75 cents, you can get a tracking number and follow the package's route to the recipient. When asked if there is anything liquid, fragile, or dangerous, always tell the postal worker that you are shipping a Prayer Shawl (or whatever it is). The people in line will hear it and it is an easy way to advertise. (The wonderful men and women at Eagle Lake's PO just roll their eyes now – they've heard about prayer shawls almost a hundred times.)

*I know this may seem a little silly God, but please
protect this package as it makes its way to the one
who needs it.*
Amen

Your personal notes:

TAGS

Colossians 4:6

Let your speech always be gracious, seasoned with salt, so that you may know how you ought to answer each person.

When you buy clothing, you look at the label for many different kinds of information – fabric content, where it was assembled, brand name, and washing instructions. You might consider putting similar tags on your shawls.

Tags can be paper or fabric and can be pinned, tied or sewn onto the garments. Two ready-made tags are your ministry's business cards and the fabric content and washing instructions on the yarn skein's sleeve.

I have also seen fabric tags which were hand sewn. These are very beneficial if the original recipient later gives the item away.

I believe it is important to let the recipients know what the fabric is – so many people are allergic to so many things! Washing instructions will make the recipient much more at ease about wearing the item. And your recipients will want to get in contact with you – either to voice their appreciation or to ask for a similar item to be sent to someone else – so your business card or brochure, attached with a large golden safety pin, makes a nice tag.

Sometimes, Lord, we overlook the final details. We are so anxious to finish the project and get it into the hands of the woman or child in need, we forget to think ahead. Help us to take a few extra minutes and take care of the little details. Amen.

Your personal notes:

BABY SWEATER

Psalm 127:3

*Behold, children are a heritage from the Lord, the
fruit of the womb a reward.*

Crochet hook size f for infant, g or j for child
Fingering yarn for infant, 4-ply sports for child
Any color or combination of colors
Buttons, snaps or ties

This sweater is an adaptation of a pattern I found in a British book. I made three of them and then got bored and started embellishing, changing the main stitch, adding this, taking that away, and trying various collars and sleeves. The instructions below will help you to do the same.

The sweater is described below in five main sections: bodice, torso, border, collar, and sleeves. Mix and match the styles to suit your needs and whims!

Colors – this sweater can be made in solid (and the first time you make it, I'd suggest you do that). If you want stripes, change the colors at the end of the row by tying off the first color and slip stitch onto that stitch after you have turned the fabric. You may also use the already striped skeins or variegated to present intriguing designs. You'll weave the ends in as you crochet the border. Trim and cuff of the sleeve should be the same color.

Bodice
Chain 48.

Working in your choice of loops (front loop gives a ribbed effect, both loops makes a smooth surface, etc.), one half-double crochet stitch in each stitch below unless otherwise stated

Row 1:
1 hdc in third chain from hook. 13 more hdc.
(1 hdc, chain 2, 1hdc) in next stitch. (1 hdc, chain 2, 1hdc) in the following stitch.
14 hdc.
(1 hdc, chain 2, 1hdc) in next stitch. (1 hdc, chain 2, 1hdc) in following stitch.
14 hdc. Chain 2. Turn

Row 2:
1 hdc in each stitch below (your choice of loops) except (2 hdc, chain 2, 2 hdc) in each 2 chain space. When you reach the end of the row, chain 2, turn.

Rows 3 – 9: Repeat Row 2.

If you are going to do Tunisian sleeves, pause at this point and go down to the instructions for Tunisian Sleeves.[T]

Row 10
Single crochet until you get to the first chain space. (SC in the chain space, skip all the stitches between the chain spaces, YO, put crochet hook into the 2nd chain space and YO. Draw hook back through the chain space. YO, draw through all loops on the hook.) Single crochet across to next chain space. Repeat directions in the parenthesis ( ). Single crochet across to end of the row. Chain 2, turn.

Row 11
Single crochet across to under arms. Decrease the two stitches – one from each side – into one. Sc 14. Decrease two into one stitch. Continue sc until there are 15 from the next under arm. Decrease two into one stitch. Sc 14, Decrease the two stitches – one from each side – into one. Sc to end. Chain 2, turn.   Bodice made.

Torso
Rows 12 – 20+ (size to fit desired length)
From this point on, you can use any stitch or combination of stitches to make your pattern interesting. HDC gives a solid, warm look. DC is not as warm, works more quickly, and is softer. SC is boring, but you can do so if you wish. DC the first three stitches of each row and the last three of each row Combinations make the sweater look interesting:

- ✓ Alternate rows of sc, hdc, and dc.
- ✓ Alternate stitches between sc, hdc, and dc and on the following row, match dc for the sc below and sc for the dc below, keeping the hdc the same. This gives a waffly look – very nice.
- ✓ Cross bars are really interesting. DC the first three stitches of each row and the last three of each row. So, the pattern for one row would be: 3 dc, skip one stitch, dc in next stitch – front loop. DC in the stitch you skipped. Skip the next unworked stitch, DC front loop, dc in the stitch you skipped. Continue to the last three stitches, which you will do as DC. The rows in between these will be straight sc in back loops.
- ✓ Using a Tunisian crochet hook, capture all of the stitches of row 12 and do a solid Tunisian stitch for the remaining rows. This is a great base if you want to embroider or cross-stitch the torso.

I've also worked the torso in shells and popcorn clusters and any other interesting stitch you can work in a straight line. If you do fancy stitches, keep the first and the last three stitches "normal".

Border
When you make your last stitch of the torso, do not finish off unless you are changing colors.
Hdc around the outside edge.
When you get to a corner, 3 Hdc in it.
Along the sides where the stitches are perpendicular to you, put three hdc in DC, two hdc in hdc, one hdc in sc.
Hdc around collar.*
Slip stitch to first hdc of the bottom row.
Finish and tie off. Weave in loose thread.

*Collar
The collar is worked as part of the trim. It can be worked these ways for various affects:
Sc = collarless
Hdc = Manchurian style collar
Dc = collar that will fold back
Tc = Ruffly collar
You can add a hood as well, but I haven't been pleased with the look.

Sleeves
Sleeves can be worked many different ways. Here are three suggestions.

From shoulder to wrist:
Start at the bottom underarm where you joined the chain spaces with the yarn-over stitches. Slip stitch to begin. HDC around. Slip stitch to first stitch, chain 2.
Continue this pattern: HDC in each stitch around, slip stitch in chain 2 space, chain 2 for each row.
Long sleeves: 9 rows of pattern or longer to match child's arm length.
Short sleeves: 3 rows of pattern.
Final row (cuff) Turn, sc around. Slip stitch to first stitch, finish off. Weave loose thread into inside of sleeve.

Or
(As attachments)
Make a rectangle of sc or hdc stitches that begins with a chain 24 (long sleeve) or 9 chain (short sleeve) and is the same number of rows as number of stitches in the armhole of your bodice. Slip stitch to join the top and bottom rows. Join with slip stitch to the y-o stitch of the bodice, slip stitch or sc along to join around the shoulder. Finish off. Weave yarn into inside of sleeve.

Or

^T Tunisian.

Single crochet until you get to the first chain space. Change your crochet hook for a Tunisian one. Do a Tunisian SC stitch through each stitch between the chain spaces. Continue the Tunisian process for fifteen rows.

Rows 16, 18, 20:

Decrease the third from the beginning and the third from the end of the row

Rows 17, 19, 21:

Do a Tunisian SC stitch through each stitch.

(adjust length of sleeves to fit by repeating the odd/even rows above)

Cuff: sc in each stitch for 3 rows. Turn, Hdc through both loops across. With right sides together, slip stitch the two sides together, moving upward to the bodice. Don't make it too tight or the sleeve will bunch.

Single crochet until you get to the next chain space. Repeat the sleeve and the cuff directions. Single crochet until you get to the end of the row. Chain 2, return to row 11 above and then begin the torso.

Closures

Sew buttons on at the places you want – in the center of the three plain dc along the trim. The other side of the flap will serve as a natural button hole because of the three plain dc stitches. Be careful about what buttons you choose. I've found that really bright and adorable ones often have warnings in tiny little letters that say they are not to be used for children under two. This means they most likely are a choking threat. If it states that it is not to be used by children under the age of seven, then it is most likely a lead-based paint problem. Some buttons can't be machine washed.

Sew them on with more loops than you would normally do; kids love to chew on things.

Snaps are easy to sew on to the posts of the three sc borders. Again, use more thread than you would normally do for an adult garment.

Ties are fun and easy to make – just chain the number you want and sc back along it. You can attach it with a slip stitch before you begin the chain and slip stitch to finish off. Make a matching tie on the other side of the torso. Keep the ties short enough so that they won't find their ways into the baby's mouths or around their necks.

Coordinate a cap and booties with the sweater and this becomes a really nice set. Add a blanket to it and you have the perfect gift.

Dearest Father,
Let the child who wears this sweater know without a
doubt that his or her parent loves them and let the
parent always remember that this child is a
beautiful gift from You.
Amen

Your personal notes:

RESALE SHOPS – TO BUY OR NOT

Ephesians 2:10
_For we are his workmanship, created in Christ
Jesus for good works, which God prepared
beforehand, that we should walk in them._

You've seen them hanging in the thrift shops and resale shops – beautiful shawls and lovingly crafted baby afghans. The yarn alone would cost five times what the shop is asking.

Do you buy it and donate it to your ministry or not?

At what point do you consider a hand-crafted item "used"?

I see nothing wrong with buying a crocheted or knitted item and donating it to our shawls or baby things. I have many wonderful hand-knitted sweaters and hand-crocheted shawls that I didn't make myself – I found them at Goodwill or Salvation Army or any number of local thrift shops. When we were making the thirty afghans for the Mary Walker House's Shelter for Women Veterans, I had antique dealers and thrift store managers who kept their eyes open for well-made afghans to add to our stock.

The items need to have no sign of wear and definitely no tears or breaks in the stitches. You can tell if a hand-crafted blanket has been washed or not. (It will **need** to be washed after you buy it.) Whoever made them would probably LOVE the idea that they would get another chance at being useful. And the money spent goes to a very good cause.

Dear Lord,
You know the needs of us all. And I have
discovered that sometimes you and I have a
different sense of time. But your sense of timing
always works to perfection. If you have blessed the
hands of other women to make shawls and blankets
and baby items in years past and you have graced
me with being able to find them when they will be
needed, keep my pride out of the picture. I don't
have to be the one who crocheted or knitted each
item in my prayer shawl ministry. I don't even have
to know who the craftswoman was. I just have to
trust that you knew and loved her, and she provided
us with what we needed, even if it was years earlier.
You knew what we needed before we knew it and
you have provided. Thank you!
Amen.

Your personal notes:

REIGNING IT BACK INTO MINISTRY

Matthew 5: 14 – 16
*"You are the light of the world. A city on a hill
cannot be hidden. Neither do people light a lamp
and put it under a bowl. Instead they put it on its
stand, and it gives light to everyone in the house. In
the same way, let your light shine before men, that
they may see your good deeds and praise your
Father in heaven."*

A good prayer shawl ministry offers women a safe place to come and discuss the stories and wisdom of their lives. It is a place where we can talk and keep up with families and events. It is a place where we can voice our frustrations and weaknesses. It is a place to share celebrations and sorrows. It is a place where women can be women first; mothers, wives, daughters and career-women second.

But sometimes – gossip slips in between the stories. Boasting outweighs the wisdom. Anger and bitterness etch along the frustrations and weaknesses. Envy and superiority shatters what blessings and healing the celebrations and shared sorrows may have given.

It always seems to creep into a meeting, like a gentle tide. Without realizing it, your circle is underwater and drowning.

Jesus stood on a boat about to be capsized and said, "Peace, be still" to the storm. As the facilitator of your circle, you need to do the same. Turn the tide of vicious gossip by changing the subject, or by deflecting it. For example, when someone says something negative about someone, counter it with something positive – even if it is hard to think of something positive about that person; "She had on the prettiest shoes last Sunday."

When one of your circle gets caught up in boasting or woe-is-meing ("I've done it better", "I had a worst time than you", etc.) state quite sweetly, "You have been through so much, and you are stronger and much nicer for it." If they hear anything other than a compliment, they will realize they've gone beyond your accepted boundaries for the group.

Don't be afraid to smack them on the nose (not physically) by changing the subject away from their control. Firmly, turn to another woman and change subjects, "That is a beautiful color yarn, what are you making it into?" Even (or especially) if it is obviously a cap or bootie, the interrupted speaker will lose their audience and the newly questioned woman will catch on and eagerly help you change the course of the conversation.

Always, always, always end your meeting with a prayer which incorporates all who were there and all who couldn't make it that meeting. Reiterate the purpose of the group. Remind them of what lies ahead. And thank God for each and every person there.

Giver of Life,
I know there is no hurt like that inflicted by a
church. I know there is no pain like that of being
gossiped about by people I believed were my
friends. I know there is no greater temptation than
to boast about bigger accomplishments or more
horrible disasters. Guide and guard the women in
this circle. Protect and preserve them. Direct and
defend them. We are here to minister to others. We
are here to fellowship with each other, to lift and
support. Give me the strength and the courage to
set boundaries and to abide by the boundaries.
Help us build friendships but also make us ministers
for your kingdom.
Amen

Your personal notes:

SETTING UP THE YEAR

Genesis 1:29

And God said, "Behold, I have given you every plant yielding seed that is on the face of all the earth, and every tree with seed in its fruit. You shall have them for food."

Every January, I begin the meeting with calendars already set. We meet every other Tuesday night, so it is easy for me to already have the dates typed up on paper ready to hand out to my ladies. I also give a copy of them to the church secretary. I post the dates on Facebook and Meet-up and on my Prayerful Shawl's blog. If you have a local paper which doesn't charge for church notices, you may consider asking them to include your meetings in their calendar of community events.

That done, you have a bare skeleton of your ministry's year ahead. Now you need to set goals and post celebrations.

In your calendar, write each member's birthday. Set up when certain projects need to be completed and what the goals for each are. For example, the first week in December, we pack up our 120 caps for Avon Park Youth Academy, so we need to have a progress check at the meetings in June and October. All three of these dates need to be posted in your calendar. Dinners need to be scheduled about every three months, with the locations listed. If you send shawls to Dover every other month, set a specific date for each time. If you have refreshments, go ahead and post who is responsible throughout the year. Pencil in when your winter visitors are heading back north or your summer visitors are heading back south.

Use your calendar like a map into a foreign country – let it keep you on the right roads toward your goals. Post it in your ministry room and continue to add to it as the year progresses.

Once the year is over, keep the calendar in with your other mementos.

Other ways to keep your members in the loop:

Email – set up a free email account. Yahoo, g-mail, Hotmail, etc all offer free email accounts. Call it by the name of your group. Chances are, the name of your group has not already been taken on one of these email servers. If it has, tweak it just enough to keep your identity without confusing your members. Every week, send your members a short note about what is coming ahead. Include a Bible verse or a hymn. Use the card function to send out birthday cards and invitations to special events. You can include other people who are not physically able to attend your meetings. Right now we have about a dozen women who attend the meetings, but two dozen people who receive the emails.

Snailmail – Not everyone is on the web. (Most of my ladies do not have email.) Remember how to write longhand on really pretty stationery? You have to address the envelopes and stick stamps on them and take them to these strange places called Post Offices. Archaic, I know, but delightful, too. Who doesn't enjoy a perky note in the midst of a dreary week?!

Social Networks – like Twitter, Facebook, Meet-up, etc. Set up accounts on these networks in the name of your group. Post to them at least once a week. Befriend people around the world who share in your group's vision and mission. You'd be amazed how many people can help and support and advertise your ministry!

Traditional News – local newspapers, church-sponsored magazines, community newsletters are all places which might post information about your group. Don't be shy about writing up news articles (inverted pyramid style works best) and attaching digital photos about the things you are doing. For the larger papers, your 100 words may just be a fluffy filler; for your group, it's that 15 minutes of glory; for strangers, it may be that one bit of news to brighten their day or that one invitation they have been hoping to find their whole life.

Yes, this all takes an incredible amount of time. Don't hesitate to delegate responsibilities. Ask for volunteers: those with beautiful penmanship – greeting cards brigade; type like a demon possessed? Social networking division. Took journalism in high school? Official journalist for your ministry. Have a digital camera somewhere? Photographer Fantastique! Don't forget to draft outlying personnel – the child who can speak computer – let them set up your websites; the husband who drives his wife to the meetings and then has nothing else to do – hand him a camera. The person who would love to come to your meetings but is 2,000 miles away – let her host one of your social networks.

Craft stores – they always have a bulletin board. Thumbtack several of your business cards there every time you go. Post one of your newsletters. Make a flyer about a special event and post it there. Don't tuck business cards or newsletters in the yarn bins – this irritates the clerks because they have to collect them and throw them away.

When you get overwhelmed, it is usually because you've drifted off the path. Regroup, re-visit your organizational notes, erase, mark out, re-write. Take a deep breathe! Pray. But don't give up. Set your ministry up one year at a time. Experience your ministry one meeting at a time. Build your ministry one prayer at a time.

Dear God,
I know that nothing can separate us from you – not
the internet, not the deadlines, not the price of
postage stamps, not the distance between our
members. Nothing can separate us from you.
Thank you!
Amen.

Your personal notes:

CROCHET HOOK SIZE SCRIPTURES

Psalm 119:105
Your word is a lamp to my feet and a light to my path.

When I was growing up, we used to memorize Bible verses in Sunday School and Vacation Bible School. I taught my elementary and middle school students to memorize famous quotations and trivial facts. About my thirtieth year of teaching, educational gurus began to proclaim that memorization and the like was "not conducive to the student's burgeoning ego." As a result, we have generations of Christians who cannot pull from their memory the very scriptures which define our faith.

Here's a little chart you may want to print up and post in your ministry room to help remember some vital Scriptures. For every crochet hook, there is a Scripture!

A. **Acts 1:14** All these with one accord were devoting themselves to prayer, together with the women and Mary the mother of Jesus and his brothers.

B. *Beatitudes* **(Matthew 5:3-10) Blessed** are the poor in spirit, for theirs is the kingdom of heaven. **Blessed** are those who mourn, for they shall be comforted. **Blessed** are the meek, for they shall inherit the earth. **Blessed** are those who hunger and thirst for righteousness, for they shall be satisfied. Blessed are the merciful, for they shall receive mercy. **Blessed** are the pure in heart, for they shall see God. **Blessed** are the peacemakers, for they shall be called "sons" of God.

Blessed are those who are persecuted for righteousness' sake, for theirs is the kingdom of heaven.

C. **II Chronicles 7:14** If my people who are called by my name humble themselves, and pray and seek my face and turn from their wicked ways, then I will hear from heaven and will forgive their sin and heal their land.

D. **Deuteronomy 7:9** Know therefore that the Lord your God is God, the faithful God who keeps covenant and steadfast love with those who love Him and keep His commandments, to a thousand generations.

E. **Exodus 35:25** And every skillful woman spun with her hands, and they all brought what they had spun in blue and purple and scarlet yarns and fine twined linen.

F. **Philippians 4:6** Do not be anxious about anything, but in everything by prayer and supplication with thanksgiving let your request be known to God.

G. **Galatians 5:22-23** But the fruit of the Spirit is love, joy, peace, patience, kindness, goodness, faithfulness, gentleness, self-control; against such things there is no law.

H. **Hebrews 11:1** Now faith is the assurance of things hoped for, the conviction of things not seen.

I. **Isaiah 55:12** For you shall go out with joy and be led forth in peace; the mountains and the hills before you shall break forth into singing, and all the trees shall clap their hands.

J. **Jeremiah 29:11** For I know the plans I have for you, declares the Lord, plans for welfare and not for evil, to give you a future and a hope.

K. **I Kings 8:28** Yet have regard to the prayer of your servant and to his plea, O Lord my God, listening to the cry and to the prayer that your servant prays before you this day.

L. **Luke 7:44** Then turning toward the woman He said to Simon, "Do you see this woman? I entered your house, you gave me no water for my feet, but she has wet my feet with her tears and wiped them with her hair."

M. **Matthew 6:5** And when you pray, you must not be like the hypocrites. For they love to stand and pray in the synagogues and at the street corners, that they may be seen by others. Truly, I say to you, they have received their reward.

N. **Nehemiah 8:10** Then he said to them, "Go your way, eat the fat and drink sweet wine and send portions to anyone who has nothing ready, for this day is holy to our Lord. And do not be grieved, for the joy of the Lord is your strength."

O. ***Our Father*** **(Matthew 6:9-13)** **Our Father** in heaven, hallowed be your name, your kingdom come, your will be done, on earth as it is in heaven. Give us this day our daily bread, and forgive us our debts as we also have forgiven our debtors. And lead us not into temptation, but deliver us from evil.

P. **Psalm 39:12** Hear my prayer O Lord, and give ear to my cry; hold not your peace at my tears! For I am a sojourner with you, a guest, like all my fathers.

Q. ***Quietness*** **Isaiah 32:16-17** Then justice will dwell in the wilderness, and righteousness abide in the fruitful field. And the effect of righteousness will be peace; and the result of righteousness, **quietness** and trust forever.

R. **Romans 12:12** Rejoice in hope, be patient in tribulation, be constant in prayer.

S. **Song of Solomon 8:7** Many waters cannot quench love, neither can floods drown it. If a man offered for love all the wealth of his house, he would be utterly despised.

T. **I Thessalonians 5:8** But since we belong to the day, let us be sober, having put on the breastplate of faith and love, and for a helmet the hope of salvation.

U. **I Chronicles 8:40** The sons of **Ulam** were brave warriors who could handle the bow. They had many sons and grandsons—150 in all. All these were the descendants of Benjamin.

V. **Vayikra 19:10** And thou shalt not glean thy kerem (vineyard), neither shalt thou gather every grape of thy kerem; thou shalt leave them for the oni (poor) and ger (stranger); I am Hashem Eloheichem. (Orthodox Jewish Bible)

W. **Wisdom of Solomon 19:22** "For in all things, O Lord, thou didst magnifie thy people, and glorifie them, neither didst thou lightly regard them: but didst assist them in euery time and place." 1611 King James Version (KJV)

X. **Esther 1:9** Queen Vashti also gave a banquet for the women in the royal palace of King **Xerxes**.

Y. **Yochanon**   **10:11**
I am the Ro'eh HaTov (the Good Shepherd). The Ro'eh HaTov lays down his neshamah for the tzon. (Orthodox Jewish Bible)

Z. **Zecharia 1:11** They reported to the angel of the LORD standing among the myrtle trees, "We have patrolled the earth, and right now the whole earth is calm and quiet."

A WORD ABOUT THANKS

Luke 17:17-18
Then Jesus answered, "Were not ten cleansed?
Where are the nine? Was no one found to return
and give praise to God except this foreigner?

I know you are not giving things away just to receive thanks from the recipients. But every now and then, it would be nice.

Don't count on it. You will get very few thank you notes. Don't despair and don't feel like your gifts and talents were wasted; they were not. Remember the situation the recipient was going through – sorrow, grief, illness, loss, pain, confusion, despair. They haven't forgotten your kindness; they were not in a place in their life at that time where they could easily and politely express their gratitude.

The goodness of your kindness will never be forgotten. It will be passed on from one person to the other, from stranger to friend to family member to stranger again and again. Kindness and love are never lost in the world. You may never hear the words, "thank you." But you will see it in every child's smile and hear it in every woman's laughter.

Dearest Giver,
Thank you. You brought me from the edge of
despair and darkness to the center of hope and
light. With every stitch that I make, let me show you
my gratitude. With every item I complete and give
away, let it take with it the love and grace you have
given me. For it is not the shawl or the blanket or
the booties that I share today, but the Love you have
first given me.
Amen.

Your personal notes:

RESOURCES

Genesis 28:15
*"I am with you and will watch over you wherever
you go, and I will bring you back to this land. I will
not leave you until I have done what I have
promised you."*

The Holy Bible, Torah, or other Holy Writings
Whichever version works for you to encourage you and others

Your church, synagogue, temple, or other sanctuary
Whichever spiritual place works for you to build comprehension and
renew compassion

The Shawl Ministry Website
www.shawlministry.com
Shawls have been made and given away for centuries. In 1998,
Janet Bristow and Victoria Galo began what is now called "The
Prayer Shawl Ministry." This website has everything you would
need to begin, develop, and continue your own ministry. They have
brochures in English and Spanish, patterns, and explanations and
suggestions for every area of your ministry. These women are
available to hold conferences and seminars. There is even a yearly
convention!

Teen Parent Centers
Along with Prayer Shawls, we make baby layettes, blankets,
booties, and caps for the two Teen Parent Centers in our county.
You can check with your local school board for the centers close to

you and get in touch with their Lead Teacher. Most of these students are between the ages of thirteen and seventeen and are pregnant but continuing their middle or high school classes in order to provide a better life for their babies than they could offer without a high school diploma.

Hospitals
Almost every hospital has a chapel. You might consider contacting the Chaplain and offering to leave a shawl-filled bag for anyone who might benefit from it. Due to privacy rules, you cannot ask who is a patient or anything else of a personal nature.

Nursing Homes, VA Centers, Convalescent Centers, and Hospices
Check your phone book or on-line search engines for local centers near you. Contact their directors and offer shawls and lap-robes to those who are interested.

Gift Tags
Gift tags can be used for many purposes other than just saying, "Here, this is for you."
On the front of my gift tags is a poem (you may use it if you keep the © by Evelyn Rainey on it). On the back of the tag is contact information and a listing of the times and dates of our meetings for the entire year. I had these laminated and attach them by means of a colorful paperclip to each shawl after we prayer over it.

May this shawl bring you
Grace in this time of difficulty,
Joy in this time of sorrow, and
Hope in this time of despair.
© Evelyn Rainey 2008

Songs to uplift and keep rhythm

There are so many types of spiritual music available today through Youtube and other online locations. Traditional hymns can be found at two wonderful websites:

Oremus Hymnal (www.oremus.org/hymnal)

Cyberhymnal (www.cyberhymnal.org)

Consider asking your church's music minister about songs with a strong rhythm.

Yarns, Patterns, and Networking

There are a great number of craft stores on and off-line. I am not ignoring them; I love my local stores and my on-line stores. However, I first learned about Prayer Shawls on one particular website: Lion Brand Yarn Company. They offer free patterns for prayer shawls which I use in my ministry. I could not end this devotional without mentioning them. **www.lionbrand.com**

2 CHRONICLES 7:14

If my people, who are called by my name, will humble themselves and pray and seek my face and turn from their wicked ways, then will I hear from heaven and will forgive their sin and heal their land.

ABOUT THE AUTHOR

Evelyn Rainey has always loved to tell stories and help others understand. As such, she is a published author and educator. But she is also the caregiver of her mother, an herb and vegetable gardener, cat wrangler, and crochet artist. Ordained as an Elder through the Presbyterian USA Church in 2010, Reverend Rainey is currently in the process of obtaining her Masters in Christian Studies through The Baptist College of Florida.

After 38 years in education, Evelyn retired, having earned degrees and certificates in Early Childhood Education, Elementary Education, Gifted Education, Integrated Middle School Curriculum, English for Speakers of Other Languages, and Journalism. She also taught all grade levels from Kindergarten through Adult and at many different facilities, including jails and teen pregnancy centers.

Evelyn has had over a dozen books published including science fiction, fantasy, historical fiction, new age urban fantasy, and children's books. She has facilitated writer groups and been guest speaker and guest author at writer conferences and conventions throughout the southeast US.

Her love of teaching has expanded into videos for book trailers, crochet lessons, meditations, and Bible studies. Her love of writing has expanded into managing ShelteringTree.Earth, LLC Publishing.

She loves corresponding with readers and authors and is available for conferences and other book events in person or through online meetings. Her website and contact information can be found on **EvelynRainey.com**.

OTHER BOOKS BY THE AUTHOR
(MOST ARE AVAILABLE AS PAPERBACK, HARDCOVER, KINDLE,
AND/OR AUDIOBOOKS)

Minna Pegeen (Comfort Publishing 2011)
Bedina's War (Comfort Publishing 2012)
Perky's Books & Gifts (Bedlam Press 2013)
    AUDIBLE: narrated by Holly Adams
The Island Remains (Whiskey Creek Press 2014)
    AUDIBLE: narrated by Ricky Tyler
Laughing Humans (Portals Publishing 2015)
    AUDIBLE: narrated by Gary Roelofs
Daisy and the Three Shoes (Gingersnap Press 2017)
Caleb's Crop (ShelteringTree.Earth 2021)
Troughton Company (ShelteringTree.Earth 2021)
Portals of Light, Doors of Despair Series
    Comes the Warrior (BLISS Books 2016)
        AUDIOBOOK: narrated by April Doty
    To Build an Army (ShelteringTree.Earth 2021)
    To Hold Back the Dark (ShelteringTree.Earth 2022)
Woven Prayers (ShelteringTree.Earth 2022)

DISCUSSION GUIDE FOR GROUP MINISTRY AND INDIVIDUAL REFLECTION

1. When did you first learn to crochet? Did it come easily or was it difficult?
2. What was the first thing you made?
3. What is the hardest thing you have ever made?
4. Be honest – how many skeins of yarn do you have?
5. Until reading this book, had you considered using your crochet hobby as a ministry?
6. Of all the patterns, what do you make most often? Why?
7. The patterns in this book are written in a non-traditional style (no secret codes or diagrams). What did you think of how they were presented?
8. Is there s particular season of the year you are most likely to crochet? Why?
9. Would you consider beginning a prayer shawl ministry? Make a plan on how you would accomplish this.
10. Did a particular devotion in this book touch your heart? Which one and why?
11. Which pattern called to you? Have you made it yet? What did you change and what did you leave the same?

12. Do you have someone you can call in the middle of the night to help you through a problem of any kind? Who, or why not?

13. Are you the kind of person one can call in the middle of the night to help them through a problem of any kind? Why or why not?

14. The next time you take your bag of crochet out in public, pay attention to how people treat you and how you react.

15. If you were asked to teach a class on crochet, what pattern would you choose? What yarn, hooks, and location?

16. Describe a crocheted item someone could make and give to you which you would absolutely love.

17. Make that item and give it to yourself.

18. Make another one and give it to a friend.

19. Make a third one and give it to a total stranger or to a thrift shop anonymously.

20. If you could sum up what you have learned in this book, what would it be?

SHELTERING
TREE

●

EARTH
PUBLISHING

We are an exclusive traditional publishing house.

Our readers, once they finish one of our books, will be
able to get up and face the world wiser, stronger,
centered, and with the assurance that we are not alone:
we are all a part of the Sheltering Tree on Earth.

If you as a writer feel that same calling, please refer to

ShelteringTree.Earth/writer-guidelines

www.ingramcontent.com/pod-product-compliance
Lightning Source LLC
Chambersburg PA
CBHW070404090426
42733CB00009B/1522